Memoirs of Laurick Ingram
(An Intimate Conversation)
A Life Story Concept
https://lifestoryconcept.com

Life is either a grand adventure or nothing at all.
- Helen Keller (1880 - 1968)

For while the tale of how we suffer, and how we are delighted, and how we may triumph is never new, it must always be heard. There isn't any other tale to tell, it's the only light we've got in all this darkness.
-James Baldwin (1924 - 1987)

Copyright © 2025
Laurick Ingram and Life Story Concept
All rights reserved.

For Tosca!

In 2023, I shared the idea for Life Story Concept with my grandniece Tosca. We decided we would develop the project together as a labor of love. Our initial plan was to interview the eldest member of families and capture their stories while they were here to tell them.

In 2024, my sweet dear niece Tosca unexpectedly left here at the age of thirty-two. Even though on her side of the family the eldest member was her grandmother Delores who was in her 80s, life took Tosca first. I still think it's important to capture and treasure the life stories of our elders, but I no longer think theirs is the only story that is important, I now understand the saying "There is no time like the present but no present like the time." While you have the time, talk to those who you love, listen deeply, learn their story then protect it and pass it on.

Preface

One of the core ideas of the Life Story Concept is "That which you think you will not forget, you may not remember, so write it down." How many people have you heard say, "I should `write a book about my life!" Maybe you have said it yourself. Then ask yourself, how many people have done it? That is where we come in. We not only slay the dragon of procrastination, but we also help you tell your story in your own voice with polish and panache. We write down and permanentize the important life experiences and memories that make you, You. We create a written legacy that can last for generations to come. A hundred years from now when your great, great grandchild is in elementary school and given the dreaded "Family Tree" assignment. She will be able to read your book and understand the breadth, depth, and scope of your life, long before she was even a notion in the minds of her mother and father.

Because we live in the age of information overload, the challenge is not gathering the information, the challenge is harnessing, organizing, and focusing the information into something that is meaningful and memorable. A hundred-watt light bulb can illuminate a small room for a short while, but a hundred-watt laser can etch your name in a bar of gold that can be passed down for generations. Your memoir is priceless and should be treasured for generations. We would be honored to help you create and celebrate that legacy.

Memory can be an unreliable, inconvenient, and sometimes contradictory witness to history. When writing memoirs, many times it is more important how something or someone was remembered and what was believed to be true than truth itself. Because we are emotional creatures our values and realities grow out of or are anchored in what we believe is true. Growing up, from my earliest memories until my teen years, I believed my mother married my father when she was fifteen and he was thirty-five. She was not his first wife. His first wife Rhoda Mae Hudson had passed away before he met my mother. He and Rhoda had two children, Harold Junior, and Betty Jean. After my dad, Harold Senior, met my mother, Arimentha Womble, they were married and my oldest brother Robert "Bobby" was born. Three things I grew up believing were that daddy's first wife died, then he married my mother, they got married and had Bobby. By the time I became a teenager, somehow, somewhere I learned that mother got pregnant when she was 13 and had Bobby when she was 14. Then she married dad when she was 15 and he was 35. I liked that my mother and father stayed married until 1973 when my father died. I wanted to wait until I was in my thirties before I got married and wanted to only be married one time. At 30 years old I got married and to date I am still married.

I formed values based on what I thought were truths. It was not until I was in my fifties that I began to ask when and where mother and dad got married; moreover, when was their anniversary? And why was Harold and Betty's mom always remembered as Rhoda Mae Hudson, not Rhoda Mae Ingram. At this point, I believe if my mother and father were married, it was at best "common law." Also, I have no proof Harold Senior ever married Rhoda. My mother and father are long gone now and, using vital records, family documents, and witness accounts to try to piece together their life stories misses so much of who they were and how they got to be how they were. I wish I had taken the opportunity that I am offering you: to capture and preserve the stories of those you love, in their voices, in the sweet now and now, while they are still with you. And long after you or your loved ones have gone on to glory, your stories can be treasured for generations.

Authors Note: As this is my story to tell and to share, I want to be respectful to others in this story who may not want to share what occurred between us. For example, my girlfriend that went with me to my aunt's house to have sex, may not want to remember that. The experience; however, profoundly affected my values on dating and my nascent values regarding love. To stay true to my life's story, while respecting others' privacy, in some instances, I will use pseudonyms or first names rather than full names.

Table of Contents
Introduction
An Intimate Conversation
Appendix – 1959…
Afterword
Acknowledgments

Introduction

Decades ago, the idea of recording the stories of my family members rolled around in my brain, and I made some efforts in that direction. In 1989 I began to document our family tree. This was before the Internet, computers, cellphones, digital pictures, AI and all the other innovations that make many parts of our lives accessible and public. I wrote out everything by hand then paid a secretary to type it out for me. I thought it was important that who we were and where we came from did not get lost forever in time. I thought my family would think it was important, and after I did it I rented a big hall and over the next few months sent letters inviting them all to a family reunion. I come from a big family, and have seven brothers three sisters, countless nieces and nephews, cousins, and in-laws. I did not even ask anyone to pay, just to show up and meet each other. Only a handful of my family member showed up. I found this disheartening, but I realized that even though I cared about who we were and where we came from others did not care. Although I kept in touch here and there with different relatives, I never attempted another family reunion. Fortunately, I can be a little anal about hanging on to things, so in 2025, thirty-six years later, I still have those typewritten pages.

As life went on, new family members were born, and older family members and their stories passed away. I still thought it important to know the stories of who we were and who we are, but I let the opportunities to record those stories slip away.

As I said, I have seven brothers and three sisters. My oldest brother, Harold Junior, was thirty-three years older than I. In the course of our lives, I had countless conversations with him about where he grew up and what he did and what my grandparents on my father's side were like. Harold's mother was my dad's "first wife," so we had different maternal grandparents. For years, I kept telling myself, I should write or record some of the conversations I had with Harold, but I never did. By the time I was born, my dad was fifty-nine and my mother was approaching forty. Both my mother's parents had passed away, so I never got to meet them nor they I.

I regret that I did not start Life Story Concepts sooner, because as Harold got older he developed Alzheimer's. I witnessed firsthand all those treasured stories and memories eaten away by the disease. By the time he died in January 2018, I was one of the few people he still remembered and recognized.

In 2023, after the idea of Life Story Concept was created, next came deciding the best way to tell the stories. Should it be written in first person? Should it be written in third person? What should be asked in the preliminary interview? What should be left out? What should be included? Because memories are often not the best witnesses to history, when the memories conflict with documented facts, do I defer to fact or include the memory?

In life there is something called analysis paralysis. It is when you get stuck on the what ifs and don't make a decision to just act. Because I had already lost my opportunity with Harold I relied on the adage that "Little things done are better than great things planned." I did not want a repeat of what happened with Harold, so I decided to just get started and figure it out as I went along. The first person I interviewed was my oldest living sibling, my brother Ronald Ingram. My first book I wrote was the *Memoirs of Ronald Ingram*. After I completed his story, I asked myself a profound question. If your life story is so important, how come you have not done your own? That being said

I put everything else on the back burner and completed the *Memoirs of Laurick Ingram.*

After completing those two books, I decided the format I would use would be the interview format. I chose this because it allows the story to be told in the person's own voice. Also, I did this because one of the things that Ronald taught me is what you believe to be true, is often more important than truth itself. That is because we act and build our values on what we believe to be true. If we believe we can never find true love, when others tell us that they have found it, we dismiss it. In my own life story, there were things I believed were true and once I became an adult, and they were not. One example is my mother told me that I was so smart I had to be moved ahead a grade. Most of my early life I thought because I was so smart that was why I was younger than my classmates. It wasn't until I graduated high school that I learned, I was not moved ahead it was just that my mother started me at school early. I'm not sure why she felt the need to tell me that, but she did. Earlier when I mentioned that my brother Harold's mother was my dad's "first wife." From my earliest memories until I was in my fifties, I would say that Rhoda Mae Hudson was my dad's first wife. That was my belief. One day when Harold and I were talking, I asked him, "If your mother was dad's first wife, how come her name was not "Rhoda Mae 'Ingraham'?" He never answered the question, but his not answering the question, answer the question. So even though for five decades I believed my father was married to my brother's mother, it was not true.

However, in the context of our life stories it is crucial what we believe to be true. Once you learn that it is not true, I think that it is a valuable discovery, but the many decisions you made based on what you thought was true still stand.

Continuing with the example of my father and marriage. I grew up being told that my father married my mother when she was fifteen and he was thirty-five. They remained married until my father passed away in July of 1973. Because of that belief, I decided that I only wanted to be married once. I would not get married young I would wait until I was in my thirties, and once I got married I wanted it to be my one and only marriage until "death do us part." Imagine my surprise, when after I asked the question about Rhoda Mae, I asked the same question about my own mother. Although mother had a version of dad's last name (Ingram), it was spelled differently from how dad's birth name (Ingraham) was spelled, There were no legal documents such as a driver's license or wedding certificate with my mother's name on them. It was not until my fifties that I realized there was no proof that my mother and father were ever married. I cannot find a wedding certificate in public records and none of my surviving siblings nor a date nor location where they were married. Therefore, my belief and getting married and staying married was based on an untruth. I still think it was a good value, and two sons and thirty-five years later I am still married.

The way I decided to write and record life stories was in the intimate conversation format. This allows the person whose story is being told to recall the key moments in their lives as they remember them. From there it is their choice whether or not they want to investigate those memories or just take them on faith.

That being said, sit back and enjoy the *Memoirs of Laurick Ingram - An Intimate Conversation*.

An Intimate Conversation

Q: What is your full name?
A: Laurick Atleston Ingram.

Q: Where were you born?
A: Opa-locka, Florida Dr. Holden's Office, 410 Opa-locka Boulevard, Opa-locka, Florida.

Q: When is your birthday?
A: Wednesday, March 11, 1959.

Q: Who were you named after?
A: My middle name is Atleston, which was my father's middle name. When I looked in the family Bible, I saw my grandfather's name was Uriah "Athleston" Ingraham. I'm not sure how it morphed into Atleston, but it did.

Q: Is anyone named after you?

A: My eldest son Joshua "Laurick" Ingram and my great-grand-nephew, Rayden "Laurick" Thomas share my name.

Q: Is there a story about your name?
A: The story I was given was that mother told her friend, Ms. Gladys that she wanted to name me LeRon. Her friend liked the name and said she was going to name her son, LeRon, which she did. Mom came up with the name Laurick but did not tell anyone until I was born.

Q: What is your mother's full name?
A: Arimentha Doretha Womble Ingram

Q: What is your father's full name?
A: Harold Atleston Ingraham according to the family Bible, but when he came from the Bahamas to America, he changed the spelling to Ingram. I am not sure why.

Q: Where was your mother born?
A: Miami-maybe. When I went to the office of Vital Statistics for Florida, they could not find her birth certificate.

Q: Where was your father born?
A: Eleuthera, Bahamas.

An Intimate Conversation

Q: What are the names of your siblings?
A: Harold "Sonny" Ingraham, Betty Ingraham, Robert "Bobby," Kelsey "Chick," Ronald, Arena "Toy," Isadore "Iz," Arnold "Noggie," Treathyl "Thyl," Chuvez "Chuck."

Q: Do you know their birthdays?
A: Yes, I have them listed on a timeline that I keep.

Q: Where was your mother and father living when you were born?
A: James E. Scott Townhomes, which were government projects, 2366 NW 75th Street, Miami, Florida 33147.

Q: What is your earliest memory of life?
A: I remember having some yellow onesie pajamas while we were still living in the Projects, which means I was younger than five.

Q: Name a childhood friend?
A: Antwan at Jackson Toddle Inn; Daryl "Juggie" in elementary school; Johnny at Holy Redeemer; and Bruce at Archbishop Curley High School.

Q: What do you remember about him / her / them?
A: I remember Antwan was dark-skinned and kept his hair cut short. We used to play on the jungle gym together.

Daryl's nickname was "Juggie," and we used to walk to school together. He was raised by his grandmother, Mae (Gramps), and lived in the house on the corner attached to Bill's Sandwich Shop. His mother's name was Deidra, and I don't remember him having any brothers and sisters. Daryl went to Liberty City Elementary, and he and I would walk to school together. Liberty City Elementary's address was 1855 NW 71st Street, so he would get to school first then I would walk the extra four blocks to Holy Redeemer, 1301 NW 71 Street.

Q: How did your mother say you were as a child?
A: I don't remember. I know I got whippings with a big black belt with a square buckle.

Q: How did your father say you were as a child?
A: What I remember most about my father was him sitting in a chair by the front window of the house staring at nothing in particular. Bear in mind, he was fifty-eight when I was born. By the time I was five, he was sixty-three. I don't remember exactly when he was committed to the South Florida State Mental Hospital, but I know he was in his sixties. When mother and I went to visit him, he called me Ronald, never my name.

An Intimate Conversation

Q: Do you remember any bedtime stories your mother or father told you?
A: Not bedtime stories, but books. *The Cookie Tree,* and *Miss Suzy the Squirrel.*

Q: Do you remember any fairy tales that you like?
A: Vaguely, Jack and the Beanstalk, but I remember the books more.

Q: Did you walk to school?
A: At Jackson Toddle Inn, a van picked us up from the Projects. After I left Jackson Toddle Inn, I walked to Holy Redeemer. In high school I caught the bus.

Q: If somebody dropped you off at school who dropped you at school?
A: Nobody dropped me off except for the one day, I asked Zip, the local drug dealer to drive me to school in his shiny maroon 67 Chevy. I knew he was a "criminal," but he always treated me like a little brother.

Q: Do you remember any of your first days at school?
A: I remember crying when Chuck graduated Jackson Toddle Inn and went on to Holy Redeemer, leaving me at Jackson Toddle Inn.

Q: Do you remember any nursery rhymes?
A: Several, *Mary Had a Little Lamb, Jack be Nimble, There was an Old Lady who Lived in a Shoe,* to name a few.

Q: Do you remember any poems?
A: As an adult, I know at least twenty-five poems. Some that come to mind are: *Invictus* by William Ernest Henly. *If*, by Rudyard Kipling. *In and Out of Time*, by Maya Angelou. *My Love is Like a Red, Red Rose* by Robert Burns. The opening and closing sonnets to Shakespeare's *Romeo and Juliet*.

As a child two poems I remember are, first:

Star light, star bright,
The first start I see tonight,
I wish I may, I wish I might,
Have the wish I wish tonight.

The other silly poem I remember, I read in a book that Isadore or Noggie brought home from the school library. It goes:

One bright day in the middle of the night
Two dead boys got up to fight.
Back to back, they faced each other.
Drew their swords and shot each other.
A deaf policeman heard the noise.

An Intimate Conversation

Came and shot the two dead boys.
If you don't believe this lie is true
Ask the blind man, he saw it too.

Q: Did you have any pets?
A: Three dogs named Cricket, McTavish, and Sage; two parakeets in college; some goldfish when I was one year sober.

Q: What games did you play as a child?
A: I would tie a towel on my neck and pretend I was a super hero; Cowboys and Indians. Hide and seek; Tag.

Q: What television shows did you watch as a child?
A: *The Flinstones, Herculoids, Space Ghost, Johnny Quest*, the Disney Movies on Sunday night.

Q: How did you mother or father discipline you?
A: Mother with the belt. I vaguely remember daddy whipping me once with a belt.

Q: Did you like elementary school?
A: In Jackson Toddle Inn, I remember students hugging a pretty kindergarten teacher on the last day of school, but when I went to hug her she pushed me away. Somehow my child's mind attributed it to my being dark-skinned since my family teased me about being so dark.

My elementary would have been Holy Redeemer because that school ran grades three through eight. This was where I began to dislike football and basketball. For recess some of the boys decided to play football. I said I knew how to play even though I did not. Holsey, was playing quarterback and threw a pass that I missed. I don't remember exactly what was said, but I know I was teased and told I couldn't play. After that, even when I made a good play, it was seen as a fluke rather than me improving.

I went out for the basketball team. The uniforms were gold with navy blue numbers. The coach's name was Wilbur. My number was 00. I was a third string guard and only put in for one game. During that game I took one shot that I missed.

I tried track, because I used to run for fun, but I can't remember why I never made the team. I used to run with team and at the end of the season, Coach Wilbur gave me a medal for the way I supported the team. The medal meant a lot to me as it was the only athletic award I won until I entered the police academy as an adult and came in first place for overall physical fitness.

Q: Did you have a best friend in elementary school?

An Intimate Conversation

A: I would say Juggie. He was younger than I was and lived in the house on the corner of my street.

Q: What family member taught you the most?
A: I would have to say Mother as she spent the most time with me, but it depends on the area:

- Toy taught me the most about cooking and unconditional love.

- Ronald about faith in action.

- Bobby about being a life learner.

- Sonny about paying bills on time and keeping my car maintained. Sonny used to say if you needed to take a sudden trip, you should be able to get in your car, turn the key, and go.

- Chick about lifting weights and the importance of exercise.

Q: What family member did you spend the most time with?
A: Other than mother, my sweet sister Toy.

Q: Can you recall a time in your life when you were afraid as a child?

A: After I saw seventeen-year-old Dan lying dead in the middle of 63rd Street. I was ten years old. Later that night I woke up and saw him standing in my living room. He was wearing the same white T-shirt and maroon slacks. He wasn't bloody, but I could see him standing there looking at me. It was my first time experiencing an intrusive image, even though I didn't know that's what it was called.

Q: Can you recall a time as a child that you were so happy you wished it would never end?
A: The Christmas when I got my metallic green, Stingray three-speed bicycle.

Q: Did you like middle school?
A: I really did not have a middle school. I went to Holy Redeemer which was a Catholic school that went from kindergarten to the eighth grade. I entered there after leaving Jackson Toddle Inn, so I came there in the third grade. I attended Holy Redeemer from the third grade through the eighth grade. After graduating the eighth grade. I went to Archbishop Curley High School, which at the time had just became co-ed. Notre Dame High School, was the all-girl high school that my sister graduated from the same year that I graduated Holy Redeemer. Hers was to be the last year for Notre Dame High School. They sold the school to a Haitian Church, and all the girls were transferred to Curley. and they

merge with Archbishop Curley to become one school.

There were some things I liked about Holy Redeemer and some things I did not like. I liked that my brother Chuck was already there, so he and I were back and school together again like we were at Jackson Toddle Inn. I did not like the uniforms so much because my friends that went to public school did not have to wear the uniforms and I felt like I would be picked on. I do not recall any particular time that somebody did pick on me because I was wearing the uniform, so it was more in my mind than in reality.

I liked the lunch that was provided. I liked recess. I liked the library. Two books that I used to read a lot when I went in the library, more accurately I used to look at the pictures, were *Pumping Iron,* a book about bodybuilders featuring Arnold Schwarzenegger: A book on the different breeds of dogs. In my childhood I had a few dogs that were mostly mixed breed mutts.

In my childhood the dogs we owned were mutts, but I so wished for a purebred German Shepherd. One time I went to the Zion Hill Baptist Church with my mother. It was a meeting, so it wasn't on a Sunday. She let me walk up the street to one of the church members' house and in his yard he had these two beautiful albino German Shepherds. I told him if they ever had puppies, I would like one of the puppies. One day, he came driving down my street in his big landscaping truck, stopped and gave me this little brown puppy. I assumed since I had asked for one of the German Shepherds, it was a purebred. My friends teased me and told me, "No way was that a German Shepherd!" Of course, they were right, and the dog was a disappointment to me. I was ambivalent about taking the dog. Because my mother was poor, she would never turn down anything offered to her whether she liked it or wanted it. She drilled into me that I should appreciate when somebody does something for me because people don't have to do things for you. For that reason, I didn't feel comfortable telling him I didn't like the dog. I asked for a German Shepherd, and I would rather him have given me nothing than to give me a mutt, thinking he was doing me a favor. All I said to him was, "Thank you," and I kept the non-German Shepherd. It would be the last dog I would own. I've never owned one as an adult nor have my children nor my wife owned any as an adult. I say as an adult because my wife actually grew up with Great Danes in her house, but once she met me; dogs were a non-starter.

An Intimate Conversation

One of the best memories I had of Holy Redeemer was that every year, when the eighth graders were graduating the seventh graders had to serve them breakfast in the "CAFETORIUM," that is actually the name that was stenciled on the building's façade. I served when I was in the seventh grade and got served when I graduated eighth grade. It was a proud moment for me.

Q: Did you ever win any awards in middle school?
A: Holy Redeemer was not a middle school, but I remember winning two awards and one quasi award. The first award I won was for track. I went out for the track team but could not do it because mom didn't have the money to buy me sneakers and the things I needed. Nevertheless, I used to run with the team in the afternoon and keep them encouraged. At the end of the season coach Wilbur was giving out medals, he gave me a medal for supporting the team. It quite moved me. I also played basketball. I was a third string guard, and my uniform number was 00 and in the entire season I played maybe two minutes in one game. I took one shot and did not make it.

The other award I won was second place in a writing competition what it means to be *Young, Gifted, and Black*. The quasi-award came when I did an art project on ecology. I copied a picture I saw in Ebony magazine onto a big poster board. The school was so impressed with it they passed it on to be displayed at the Public Library on 62nd Street and 6th Avenue.

Q: Name one thing you got in trouble for when you were in middle school?
A: At Holy Redeemer one thing I got in trouble for was when another student named Michael said something to me in class and we got into a shoving match. We were sent down to the principal's office and Sister Clementine, the principal, Made both of us sweep the two-story staircase with a toothbrush. I remember it to this day.

Q: Can you describe a fond memory from middle school?
A: Sure, I remember going to the movies to see *The Bible* at the Bal Harbor Theater. I liked movies for a couple of reasons. One was that my sister Toy (Arena) liked movies and at home I would get to sit and watch them with her, which I enjoyed. She would mesmerize me with backstories about the actors and actresses. Trivia such as Tony Curtis's real name was Bernard Schwartz and Cary Grant's real name was Archibald Leach. Also, since I grew up pre-cable, movies were a rare treat and any time I got to go it was a special day. Whether I was going to the "Shack" theater on 15th Avenue, or catching

An Intimate Conversation

the bus downtown with my older sister, Thyl; not only would I get to see a movie, but afterwards I would get a Whopper from Burger King.

Another time was when Thomas, the police officer who lived up the street from me, let me tag along with him to his Off-Duty job at the Miami Theater. It was the weekend, and he worked extra-duty at the theater. He let me ride with him downtown, and I got to hang out in the theater for the entire day. Back then, movies showed double features, so I got to watch two movies twice and at the end of the day, I rode home with him. As if that were not great enough, because I was with him, they let me in free.

My top two movie experiences was when I went to see *Peter Pan* at the Olympia theater at night. My brother, Noggie (Arnold) took me and my brother Chuck (Chuvez), and it was our first ever nighttime movie.

Finally, first place goes to my mother. Sometimes she would get dolled up. Put on a dress and makeup and we would catch the 25 bus from 65th Street to Downtown Miami. The two movies I remember seeing with her were *Cotton Comes to Harlem* a big screen version of a Chester Grimes novel, about two New York police detectives in Harlem in the 60's. The other was *Salt and Pepper* with Sammy Davis

Junior and Peter Lawford. They played night club owners who were pseudo spies.

Q: Did you like high school?
A: To begin with, it wasn't high school, it was high schools, plural. I began my ninth grade year at Archbishop Curley High School, which had just gone co-ed. Previously, it was all boy. It was a Catholic School, and I was a confirmed Catholic. My brother Chuck was already there and went to the tenth grade as I entered the ninth grade. The way I became Catholic was, when Chuck and I were at Holy Redeemer the tuition was less if you were Catholic. It's still a mystery to me where mom got the money to send us considering some months our lights or water were turned off for nonpayment. I remember, in the way that a kid remembers, that we were no longer on welfare. Dad was not working, and mom was working as a seamstress from home. Somehow, some way, she kept Chuck and me in Holy Redeemer until we graduated.

Thyl also went to Holy Redeemer before going to The Academy of Notre Dame, where she was a straight "A" student. From there she got a scholarship, that along with financial aid allowed her to attend the University of Miami, where she got her four-year accounting degree in three years.

An Intimate Conversation

A side note here. My brothers and I used to joke about which brother was the smartest. I was never in the running, and the majority voted that Chick was the smartest. I don't remember which tests were administered to him in elementary school, but I remember my brothers and later Chick's friends saying he had darn near perfect scores across the board. I do remember when he was older, he would read logic and philosophy books for recreation. *Yikes!*

Chick ended up dropping out of high school but ultimately got his high school diploma when he joined the U.S. Air Force. When I think back on it, I suspect my brother was a brilliant as he was tortured. The odd thing is that it wasn't until I was in my fifties that I realized if you asked me that again, I would have said, none of the brothers, buy my sister Thyl was the smartest. She was a Straight A student dating all the way back to kindergarten. To my knowledge, she never got in trouble. She played the piano; could cook and sew. She took French for four years in high school and aced it every semester. I also remember her teaching herself to play one song on the guitar. I am ashamed that my male-centric vision did not even let me consider her when she was clearly the most gifted. Thyl went on to get a job with the federal government, get married, and have ten children. On the latter, she took after our mother.

Q: What are some things you did and did not like about high school?
A: Again, it was high schools, not high school.

Ninth Grade
I will start with Archbishop Curley. I made friends with another student named Bruce. A couple of times after school I went over to his house. He was an only child and by my standards he was "rich." He was raised by a single mother, but she did not look like any of the single moms I had ever seen. She was a knockout. He was sensitive about it and did not like when his friends commented on how good she looked, so after the first time I stopped mentioning it. She drove a luxury car, a Lincoln Continental I believe. Bruce not only had his own room, but he also had posters, a stereo, and hanging beads to make a faux door. On the last day of school, he and I rode our bikes to school. We were released early, and we rode all the way out the Rickenbacker Causeway, which led to Virginia Key Beach. I would have gone to the beach, but we would have to have pedaled across an elevated bridge, and I was afraid, and we turned around. One of my first negative memories of Archbishop Curley was that entering freshmen had to get on their knees and kiss

An Intimate Conversation

the school seal. I did it but found it humiliating. Prior to high school, I was a solid B student, but high school gave me some courses that required study. Although I liked to read, I did not like reading schoolwork. I fared well in English and Latin because of Sister Margaret. She was a nun that used to wear regular dresses instead of the traditional habits for nuns of her order and used to ride her bicycle to the school. She had such a passion for teaching and an unabashed concern for the students. I got B's in her class. Where I fell down was in Religion, Algebra, and Social Studies. I remember Father Berger teaching Religion. One thing I remember was his effeminate mannerisms. This was before I had ever heard of a gay priest, so I didn't know how to describe it. He never did anything to me, nor anyone I knew, so this is not a dig, it is a simple recollection.

The thing he did that stung me, had nothing to do with his mannerisms, but his lack of racial sensitivity. One day he was teaching on what it was like to be lonely. He said loneliness was such a prevailing malady that there was currently a popular song about it. "Does anyone know the name of the song?" He asked. My hand shot up because I knew I had this one. He called on me, and I answered, "*I've Been Lonely for So Long*." He frowned, flicked his hand, and said, "No." Then another kid, said, *"Alone Again Naturally,"* by Gilbert O'Sullivan. And he exclaimed, "That's it!" The thing was the song I knew was a hit for black people and although I was vaguely familiar with Gilbert O'Sullivan, his song was by no means popular in my world. I think I would have felt better if he hadn't been so dismissive of it. However, if memory serves there were fewer than twenty-five African American students in a school of more than 600 students.

Another shameful memory was during a pep-rally, I dressed in a diaper and was "Baby Knight," the Knights were the school mascot. I came out with a sword and a shield and vanquished the mascot for the opposing team. I still remember Holsey, a classmate asking me why I let them humiliate me like that. I don't know that I had a good answer.

My brother Chuck played junior varsity football at Curley, which was sensible since he was husky and liked watching the football highlights on the weekend. He injured his leg during a game or practice and had to be taken to the hospital. I am not sure why, as we never discussed it, but that was the last year Chuck played. I finished my freshman year at Curley with my first D on a report card. It was in Social Studies.

An Intimate Conversation

There was a cluster of us that had come over from Holy Redeemer, both in my class and my brother's class that had decided we had had enough of Archbishop Curley. When Chuck and I asked mom if we could transfer to public school, she said, "Yes," without any discussion. I don't know if I knew it then or figured it out later that it was because she didn't have the money. I was not sure how she was paying it in the first place, but our leaving had to be a big load off her shoulders.

Tenth Grade
For my tenth grade year and Chuck's eleventh grade year, we transferred to Miami Springs High School. Because the school was not in our neighborhood we had to catch the school bus. My memory is foggy here, because I knew Chuck and I were both there, but I don't remember us catching the school bus together. More often than not, Chuck lived with Aunt Bern. I think Aunt Bern bought him a white Pontiac Catalina and because Aunt Bern did not drive, he had to take her to work over in Bal Harbour then drive to school.

In the tenth grade at Miami Springs, I progressed, rather devolved, from getting my first "D" to getting "F's" and failing classes. Even though mom was in her fifties, life had been hard for her. Daddy had been committed to a state hospital, for what I now know was Alzheimer's; I was the last of nine children she had given birth to, not counting the three stillbirths. My daddy had two other children, Harold and Betty, but mother did not raise either of them. Harold (Sonny) was raised by his grandmother, while Betty was raised by dad's sister, Aunt Mae, and her husband, Uncle Charlie. Either way, after having given birth to twelve children and having raised nine, mother had burnt out. In a lot of ways, I was allowed to fend for myself. She did the initial paperwork that got me into Miami Springs, but after that I don't remember a single time she came to the school. The two classes I failed in the tenth grade were English and Physical Education, my second and third period classes. I failed English because I just didn't do any homework and stop attending. I failed physical education because I was being bullied by a student named Jorge. I was rail thin, weak, and sucked at most sports. My solution was to not go to the class. Also, there was a pronounced difference in Curley and Miami Springs. At Curley, if you were ten minutes late, they would call your home to ask where you were. At Miami Springs, even if you didn't show up, nobody called home. This meant I could skip school, and mom wouldn't know until the end of the semester. Part of my faulty thinking here was that mom used to tell me, "If you don't want to go to school, stay home. I don't have a car, and I don't have any money, so if you get in trouble I cannot come get you and cannot help you. I'd rather you just stay home then go out there and get in trouble." Some days I took her up on it, but hanging around the house with your mother is not nearly as exciting as wandering the streets of Miami and seeing what sort of trouble you could get into. Two of my classmates that could handle Jorge were Pretty Boy Floyd and Meadowlark. Pretty Boy didn't so much bully Jorge as let Jorge know that he was the "Alpha" in the relationship. Meadowlark, who was jet black and built like a brick wall, enjoyed letting Jorge know he was in charge. During the wrestling blocks Meadowlark would pick Jorge and manhandle him. Jorge would, in turn, pick me and manhandle me. The best thing I learned in P.E. had nothing to do with the teacher. There was a white kid, who was around my height and weight. He didn't look particularly athletic. During the block on tumbling, we were doing handsprings. I was too afraid of falling and failing to even try. Coach Steve, the overweight, cigarette smoking P.E. teacher shook his head in disgust when I was too afraid to even try. That white kid; however, kept trying and kept landing flat on his back, until one day he got it. He did a successful handspring and landed perfectly on his feet. It was an object lesson in what you could achieve if you didn't give up. Outside of P.E., Jerry, a varsity football running back, got me in his crosshairs. I think it had to do with me being friendly with his cheerleader girlfriend. I was friendly, but I didn't feel like I was a threat because I felt like she was out of my league. I guess he saw it differently and would find me in the cafeteria and the hallways between classes to try and pick a fight. Since I didn't think I could beat him in a fight, I thought it smarter to avoid him. To my detriment, I avoided him, English, and P.E.

Q: Did you ever win any awards in high school?
A: I did not win any awards that I recalled at Archbishop Curley. I did not win any awards at Miami Springs. The only positive recollection I have of Miami Springs was being in a talent show with one of my brother Chuck's friends named Carl. Carl did not win the talent show but we got a lot of laughs off the skit. Carl later went on to be a radio announcer. Because he was chubby his nickname in high school was pork chop, so he carried that to the radio station, and he would introduce himself as saying, "This is the Chops, go…

After failing the tenth grade, I once again asked mother if I could switch schools and so she allowed me to transfer to Miami Central. Chuck remained at Miami Springs so that was the last time I attended a school that he attended.

An Intimate Conversation

Ten Pushups

Something happened in Springs that altered the trajectory of my high school life. My brother Chick asked me to do ten pushups, and I could not. Going forward, he told me he wanted me to do ten pushups every day. He also told me to eat more. A few days later he showed up at the house on 65th Street with a 110 pound set of cement weights. He gave me what was called the basic six exercises: squats, biceps curls, triceps curls, overhead presses, bent over rows, and bench presses. He told me to do ten reps and four sets of each five days a week. In the tenth grade I was 5'9," weighed 159 pounds, and could not do ten pushups.

Following Chick's suggestions, I continued doing ten pushups a day and lifting weights in our backyard five days a week. I also began eating enough for two people. It was nothing for me to eat four slices of toast, three eggs, and a quart of milk for breakfast. By the time school started in September, I had packed on twenty-five pounds of muscle.

Summer School at Miami Central

I'm sorry let me back up here, but once mom let me transfer to Miami Central, I went to summer school there. I had four hours of P.E. and one hour of English. P.E. was basically volleyball for four hours, which strangely enough I end up being good at. Now this also happened after I had begun lifting weights and doing pushups which caused my physical abilities to improve. For the English class I also scored an A and learned a life lesson about cheating. Miss Irene gave a test, and I answered all the questions but there was one I was not sure about. She left the class to go and do something, and another student I believe his name was Fred, went up to her desk and read out the answers. The question I was not sure about, I changed the answer based on what Fred had read out. It turned out I was right, and the teacher had made a mistake on her answer key. She also said since everybody seemed to have gotten a near perfect score in the class including the wrong answer to the question that was an error, she threw the test out. To my recollection, that is the one and only time I ever cheated in school, whether I was making A's or failing, I would just take it rather than cheat.

Miami Central

When school started in September, I now weighed about 185 pounds, could do about 40 pushups, and felt much better about myself. I did not have to take P.E. anymore because I made up the credits during the summer. I still had to make up some English credits, and I ended up going to night school.

Because of where they lived, some of my classmates from Holy Redeemer went to Miami Central. Gregory, Lawrence, Diane, Linda, Deborah, and Reggie, come to mind. This would be my first academic opportunity to define myself. When I told mom I did not want to go to Miami Springs anymore, the area we lived in would have caused me to go to Miami Northwestern. She did not want me to go to Northwestern because Northwestern had a history for fights. Also, Chick, Ronald, Toy, Isadore, and Noggie, went to Northwestern. Toy and Ronald were the only two to graduate. Chick, Isadore, and Noggie, dropped out. What mom did not know was that I didn't want to go to Northwestern anyway. I had had enough of bullying and did not want to test waters in a school with a reputation for fights. One of my friends named Roger, was already going there. He had gotten into a fight, and the kid hit him in the face with a chair, leaving Roger with a permanent scar under his right eye.

The Double-Promotion Lie
For most of my academic life, my mother told me I had gotten a double promotion, which explained why I was a year younger than most of my classmates. I believed her and consequently believed it when she told me that I was so smart I had to be moved ahead a grade. Long after I

graduated, I learned that I was not put ahead, Mrs. Ida Bell, the owner of Jackson Toddle Inn, let mom start me when I was four instead of five-years-old. In addition to being chronologically younger than my peers, I was small even for my age, which gave me a double whammy.

When I started my eleventh grade year at Miami Central, thanks to Chick, Weider Weights, and eating like a bear, I was not only the same size as my classmates, but I was also bigger and stronger than many of them. Nevertheless, to quote Yogi Berra, "It was *déjà vu* all over again." Shortly after I arrived at Miami Central, Gregory, one of my Holy Redeemer classmates, said that one of the school's football players named Daryl had been asking about me. I had no clue who he was or what he wanted with me, but Greg told me it didn't sound good. Given my new found size and strength, I told Greg, "Okay, he knows where to find me." Greg told me you may not want him to find you. Well, I was bigger and stronger than I had been, but Daryl was a beast. Also, even though I was bigger, the "ninety-pound weakling" inside me still lacked physical confidence. When I finally saw Daryl, he was as Greg described, "a beast." We never had any classes together, so our interactions would be in the hallway. I caught him watching me a couple of times and stalking me to see if I would go to the bathroom. The bathrooms were a good place to start a fight because there were no witnesses. I had had enough of being bullied and I wasn't about to switch schools again. I came up with a plan. I got a locker in the hall on the top row. The locker beneath it was vacant. This was long before there were metal detectors in schools. One day, I smuggled an eighteen inch metal pipe into the school and hid it in the vacant locker beneath mine. Daryl was bigger and stronger, but I figured the pipe would make up for the difference. One day, I saw him angling towards me in the hall. I positioned myself by my locker where I could get to the pipe quickly. When he got close, I gave him dead eyes, and we had words. I don't remember what was said, but I know he never bothered me again. When I finally unraveled the mystery, it turns out, he liked a student named Diane, but she did not like him. Rather than just tell him she didn't like him, she told him she had a boyfriend named Laurick. Diane and I had been classmates and Holy Redeemer, and I slow danced with her and my eleven-year-old birthday party, but I had not even spoken to her since we left Holy Redeemer. Either way, being the target of bullying was done for me.

A Rocket for Life
I went to Archbishop Curley, and I went to Miami Springs, but I am a Miami Central Rocket for life.

So many things there changed the trajectory of my life. One thing was another of my classmates from Holy Redeemer, Reggie, attended Central. Reuniting with Reggie gave me a new best friend. He was brilliant, had a razor-sharp wit, and was incredibly fast. He was tall and rawboned, but he didn't have a mean bone in his body. In his junior year, he tried out for quarterback. Something happened during one of the practices that put him on the wrong side of, guess who, Daryl. It ended up with Daryl body slamming him. I didn't see it, but that is how Reggie described it. I don't know if that was the only reason, but it was part of the reason he quit the team. He wanted to be a doctor, and his grades gave him a good shot at college. Both his parents were nurses, which gave him some medical insights. He never became a doctor, but it had nothing to do with his not being smart enough. Some other challenges beset him, but that is his story to tell not mine.

Q: Name one thing you got in trouble for when you were in high school?
A: The first thing that comes to mind is something I got away with but should have gotten in trouble for.

An Orange and Black Football Jersey
In the ninth grade, I wanted an orange and black football jersey, so I snuck into the locker room

An Intimate Conversation

during lunch break. I knew the football players had separate cages that were not locked. This was so the trainers good get to the uniforms to wash them. I went in and snagged one of the jerseys, then put it in my P.E. locker. I planned to get it after school. The principal, Father Engbert, saw me going into the locker room and followed me. By the time he came in, I had hidden the jersey in my locker. He came up to me and with one hand on each side, he cinched the skin around my ribs in his fingers. He had a reputation for doing that and it hurt like heck. He asked me what I was doing in there and I told him I had forgotten one of my books when I left P.E. I had a book in my hand, because I made sure to forget it and give myself an excuse to go into the locker room. I never got caught for stealing the jersey, but it was something I did wrong.

A fact versus fiction experience I had a Curley came because my brothers and friends told me that white kids were afraid of black kids. I thought this gave me *bona fide* street creds as a *badass*. It did not. Not only were the students not afraid of me, but the P.E. coach and many of the kids bullied me. For some strange reason, I decided to be a water boy (which is how I knew about the football players' lockers). The Head Trainer, pseudonym for "Head Water Boy," was a tall effeminate guy, whose name I can't remember. I do remember us having an argument and got in his face. He shoved me so hard, I flew across the locker room and crashed into the washer and dryers. So much for white kids being afraid of us.

About the only good think I remember taking away from Archbishop Curley was the skills I learned in typing class. It did not hurt that the typing teaching was a buxom brunette named Miss Alt. Even if I hadn't cared about nor had an aptitude for typing, Miss Alt was beautiful and treated me like she was glad I was there. Other than Sister Margaret, I felt that the other teaches could have cared less whether if succeeded, failed, or showed up at all. With the advent of computers, AI, and voice recognition dictation software, typing is not nearly as important as it was back then. Typing; however, has been cornerstone of my success in school once I decided to succeed; an incredible asset in college and on the police department. That skill has been an indispensable asset in my life, as evidenced by me typing the memoirs you are reading.

Q: Can you describe a fond memory from high school?
A: Most of the fond high school memories happened at Miami Central.

Fond Memories from my Days at Central

An Intimate Conversation

- Spending time at Angela's house and swimming in the backyard lake.

- Swinging off a rope and splashing into Twin Lake.

- Marrying Vivian during Sadie Hawkins week.

- Being the emcee for the Miss Miami Central Pageant.

- Going to Washington DC for Project Close Up – A program designed to let high school students see how the government is run.

- Some parts of Project Upward Bound – A program that let high school students live in college dorms and take classes. This was to give the students a preview of what college would be like. I attended Florida Memorial College, but I heard they offered it at other colleges as well.

- Graduating early, actually finishing school early because I did not march. I did not want the drama of my mother screaming at me.

- Being a member of the CHIC, Cultural Human Interactions Committee, ran by two graduate students named Bob and Miguel.

- Watching Mr. Lester, my math teacher, do one armed pushups.

- Driver's Education. I had already been driving since I was fourteen, so the class was an Easy A.

- Making the principal's honor roll in twelfth grade.

- Arm wrestling Mr. Kent, our school's activities director and a former marine. It was a draw, and he told me, "I thought I could take you." I told him, "I thought you could too."

- Psychology class, because the teacher who knew my brother Bobby, liked me and I understood the work. By then Bobby had gone back to college while working full time and raising a family. He earned his Ph.D. and was now Dr. Ingram.

- Being appointed to the student advisory committee. Part of my assignment involved writing an editorial for the school newspaper. I learned that there were exhaust fans for the kitchen that had never been installed. I put some thermometers in the kitchen and measured temperatures of 110 degrees. I interviewed the principal about it and before I could write the article, within a week the fans were installed. I became the darling of the ladies in the cafeteria, which is why I am a big fan of peanut butter cookies to this day.

- Doing pizza run's for the night school teacher, Ms. Yvonne. She was my teacher during my regular school hours, but she also taught night school from 5 p.m. to 8 p.m. Sometimes, she would treat the night school class to pizza.

Q: Have you ever had anything stolen from you?
A: Yes, my high school ring and my brand new sneakers from Arcola Lakes Pool. My high school ring was stolen when I was living with my sister Toy. After Toy had been at the post office for a few years, she and a lady bought a house together. Toy let me come and stay there, but I think her roommate resented my being there and stole the ring out of spite.

How I loss the sneakers was one day me and some of the kids in the neighborhood walked to Arcola Lakes Park. Mom had just bought me a pair of navy blue sneakers that I could not wait to show off. When we got to the pool, I did not have enough money to rent a lock for the locker, so I just placed them in the locker without a lock. When I came back, they were gone. I had to walk three miles home in bare feet.

Q: Were you ever in a car accident as a child?
A: Yes, my sister Betty got into a car crash, and I was in the car. I think she had to get stitches across her forehead, and I bit through my tongue during the impact.

Q: Can you swim? If you can, who taught you and when did you learn?
A: Yes. I don't' remember how old I was, but I remember Isadore and Noggie throwing me in the canal behind Aunt Bern's house and figuring I would learn. It half worked. I learned enough to get back to shore.

I remember being in a summer program at the University of Miami. There a lifeguard named Dell, spent time teaching me how to swim and dive.

Q: Did you have any surgeries as a child?
A: No, but I suffered from nose bleeds.

Q: Do you have any childhood scars? If you do how did you get them?

An Intimate Conversation

A: I have a couple: I have a triangle on my left forearm which is when I got burned by an iron. And I have scars on my right knee from when I was learning how to ride a bike and fell on the street.

Q: Do you remember your kindergarten graduation?
A: I do remember my kindergarten graduation. my two front teeth were missing because when I look back at the picture I see my big toothless smile right up front when I'm singing a song with a few of the other kids. One of the songs I remember singing was *Chim Chim Cher-ee* from Disney's Mary Poppins.

Q: What do you remember about your middle school graduation?
A: I did not have middle school but went to Holy Redeemer from the third grade to the eighth grade. And I've already covered a few things that I remember about the graduation, but I also remember that my mother made my suit. It was a navy blue suit. The thing about it is my mother was a gifted seamstress but not a tailor so many of her outfits that she made for boys were a little bit off in terms of the cut of it and things like that. I remember I had a light blue shirt and a white necktie, but my mom did make the suit from scratch, and it bagged a little.

Q: What do you remember about your high school graduation?

A: What I remember about my high school graduation is not going to it. I remember taking my high school pictures but not ever buying them, consequently I am in the yearbook, but I don't have any of those pictures. I chose not to march even though I finished one semester early, which is impressive considering I was coming back from having failed the tenth grade. But most of the milestone events in my life, graduations, proms, Grad Nite at Disney World, were polluted by anger and screaming by my mother. As I reflect on it I believe it's because she was short on money and all of these things put a push on her causing her to have to ask others to help sponsor those events. When it came to graduation I simply said I'm not going to do it and then I wouldn't have to deal with that. As an adult I regret that, and I feel like I owed it to her because I was her last child to finish high school, and I thought it would mean something to her to see me march. Ronald however said that when mom came to his graduation she looked as though she couldn't wait to leave there. So whatever narrative I have in my mind is hypothetical. For my own self I wish I had marched which is why when I finished Miami-Dade and got my associates degree I made sure I marched.

An Intimate Conversation

Q: Have you ever broken any bones?
A: I have never broken any bones, I have dislocated my wrist, I have sprained and strained muscles, I fell off a ladder and hurt my back, but I never broke anything.

Q: What subject did you like in school?
A: The two subjects I liked in high school were Psychology and English. Psychology because the psychology teacher knew my brother Bobby (Dr. Ingram) and she liked me. The first day of class she asked, "Does anybody know the names of any psychologists or psychiatrists?" I said Doctor Eric Byrne. She asked me, "What is he known for?" I answered Transactional Analysis, which is a theory of psychology that says people operate from three modalities. Parent, Adult, or Child." She looked stunned that I knew it and asked me where I learned it. I told her I read a book from my brother's library. Turns out she knew my brother, and I'm sure some of it had to do with my work and grasp of the concepts of Psychology but I was a straight A student from that day forward. The other was English on a couple of levels. One was because I like writing as I already said, even at Curley when I learned how to type that helped me quite a bit. The other was that I like reading, and even though I failed English at Miami Springs and got a D in Social Studies and Curley, I read a lot of books on

my own that had nothing to do with school. I give my mother credit for that because she started me reading very early.

I liked English because I seem to have a knack for it, even during the summer at Central when I scored my first A in high school English. From there, my affinity for English was reinforced by English teacher Ms. Yvonne who was a tall, thin waisted, cappuccino complexioned, beautiful woman from Tuskegee, Alabama. I explained to her my situation that is that I had failed the tenth grade and that I would have to go to night school to be able to graduate on time. It turned out that she was the night school teacher. Much to my surprise, most of the assignments she gave I finished quickly and the few times she would call on me I actually knew the answers. Years later I would talk with Ms. Yvonne, and she shared with me that she had a special affection for me, Reggie, and Angela. It had to do with the fact that she allowed her mother to raise her own child and was not there for her own son. Ms. Yvonne taught me not only about English but much about life, she was encouraging and a bright star leading me towards success.

Another memorable teacher was Mr. Lester. He taught me Algebra and Trigonometry. He was a retired veteran and even in his fifties could do one arm pushups. He was also the first avowed atheist I ever met.

Q: What subject did you get good grades in?
A: I do not remember what subjects I got good grades at Holy Redeemer. I know I got good grades, and by that I mean B's in English and Latin at Archbishop Curley. In Miami Springs I don't remember what my report card was other than failing English and P.E.

When I got to Miami Central I got A's in English across the board and also in Psychology I got enough A's to make the honor roll. Mr. Lester, my math teacher was a critical part of my making the honor roll. I had taken Algebra and did well in it, so they moved me to Trigonometry. I realized that I could not master Trigonometry without doing homework and I didn't do the homework. What Mr. Lester did for me was, at the end of the semester, rather than give me a D or a low grade in Trig, he took me down to a math teacher that taught a lower level of math. He asked that teacher to please allow me to be on his roll and give me a B. The teacher agreed and gave me a B, which allowed me with my other grades to make the honor roll. I remember that teacher because he and his wife both worked at the school. I remember hearing that their child needed a kidney, and the wife donated one of her kidneys to their child. Even my high school limited brain, saw that as an extraordinary act of love.

Washington DC
Mr. William taught Social Studies at Central and this time I was making A's and B's. I had heard that Sister Margaret, my English teacher from Curley had requested a dispensation from her vows as a nun, so she could get married. Similar to her story, Mr. William left the priesthood to marry. He was a clean shaven man in his fifties who had a calm, reassuring manner about him and favored bowties. The school was offering a one week trip to Washington DC for students to see how the government worked. I knew my mom could not afford it, but they were offering scholarships to students who were doing well in Social Studies and American Government. I interviewed for a scholarship and Mr. William was the interviewer. He asked questions about how the government ran; the difference between the legislative executive and judicial branches; and other relevant questions pertaining to the U.S. government. I did not know some of the answers, but Mr. William would say, and you know that the president is in the executive branch, don't you? I would say, "Yes." He would check a box. I did get to DC on the scholarship, and we took field trips to the different parts and buildings of government, but honestly I couldn't

remember a single thing. What I do remember is a student named Hope, a White girl from another school. One day she and I were the first to get on the bus that was taking us around and we were on the back seat. I laid my head on her lap, and she bent over and kissed me on the lips. From there, we set a date to meet in the basement of the hotel where we kissed as much as we could. I never saw Hope again, but I treasure that memory. It was also the first time I drank beer away from my mother. I want to clarify that mother didn't give me cans of beer but sometimes she let me sip out of her can. Some other students had managed to smuggle in some Coors beer, and I got a can.

One day in the hotel's lobby, I saw Reverend Jesse Jackson at the front desk. I went up to speak to him, and he did not respond in fact he was rude. I walked away disappointed and went into the hotel gift shop. He found me in the gift shop and asked me where I was from, but my feelings are so hurt from the rebuff then now I chose to be rude to him. I regret my behavior and moreover I regret the loss of a great opportunity that was given to me to talk with a great man.

An Aptitude for Science
I enjoyed Biology class and was a consistent B student. I even enjoyed dissecting frogs. The

Science teacher was a pretty and petite white female with blonde hair. I don't remember her name, but I liked her class. From then on I actually would get good grades in Science in college as well. I guess I had an aptitude for science; not that I wanted to do anything with science as a job, but it interested me. In fact, one of my work study jobs has been a biology lab for Mr. Hap and I did very well there.

Q: What subject did you get poor grades in?
A: Trigonometry comes to mind. Although I understood the concepts in Trigonometry I rarely did any homework which kept me behind. I remember being particularly fascinated by three-dimensional graphs, which have an X, Y, and Z axes. That was Mr. Lester's class. Coincidentally, when I went to Miami-Dade college I had Mr. Lester's Brother for Biology. His brother was also an atheist and told me that he believed that within the next ten years we would know where life originated from. That was about forty years ago, and I don't think science is any closer to explaining the origin of life.

Q: Name the teacher you remember influencing your life?
A: Ms. Yvonne hands down. She encouraged me and did wonders for my esteem. She told great stories. Every year the English teachers were given

these big boxes of English books for course study because the companies wanted them to endorse the product and get the school to buy them. I remember her giving me one of those full kits to teach English for a year. She actually invited me over to her house for dinner to meet her boyfriend, who I thought was a little older than she was. Another student named Eddie. was also invited to that same dinner. Eddie was unabashedly gay at a time when a gay person was really looked down on, and gay boys were teased and taunted. I remember the night at the dinner when we were leaving her apartment, and the elevator came, and he got in, and I was afraid to get into the elevator with him. Nothing about him was threatening, but I was afraid. I remember once in a later discussion Ms. Yvonne telling me that he had been raped and that was as traumatizing for him as it would have been for any girl. I wasn't quite sure what to do with that, but it did let me know of the different types of hatred that exist in the world and how people will harm others who are different.

Q: Describe the teacher and what effect he or she had?
A: I had a teenage crush on Ms. Yvonne, and wrote a paper to that effect, which I turned in to her. I think she read it and just never commented on it because she was smart enough to know not to comment on it. Her intelligence, her confidence, her beauty, her

unabashed blackness made me believe there was a better life out there than being poor and remaining in the ghetto. I kept in touch with her over the years. Long after I left Miami Central, many times, I would see her and her best friend Ms. Bessie at the Annual Jazz in the Gardens Festival in Miami Gardens, Florida. After I became a police officer I went back and spoke sometimes to her classes. The year she taught me was her first year at Miami Central and that was her one and only teaching assignment. She retired as a teacher from Central. I think she did over thirty-five years. I even gave a scholarship in her name at my church to show her how much I appreciated her role in my life.

Q: Were you ever bullied in school?
A: I already described how I was bullied in the ninth, tenth grades, until I put the kibosh on it in the eleventh grade.

Q: Were you ever a bully in school?
A: No, I did not like it being done to me and doing it to someone else did not appeal to me.

Q: Were you ever in any plays or music programs?
A: In kindergarten I know we sang it graduation and did the kindergarten shows, but I don't believe I was ever in any music programs. Holy Redeemer had a band, and I wanted to play the flute but once my

mom saw how much a flute cost, said absolutely not. Other than the brief skit at Miami springs with Carl Trammel, that was the extent of my participating in plays or music programs.

Q: Have you ever performed anywhere?
A: I was the master of ceremony for the Miss Miami Central pageant, a definite high point of my high school career. Mother actually attended the show.

Q: Were you baptized? Do you remember where you were baptized? And who baptized you?
A: I was baptized five times.

Baptisms
The ones I remember clearly are Saint James Methodist Church, Mount Tabor Baptist Church, Holy Redeemer Catholic Church, and the Church of Christ I joined at the behest of my sister Thyl.

I'll talk about a Holy Redeemer first. The reason I became a Catholic was that even though a non-Catholic could attend the school, if you were a Catholic the tuition was discounted. I became a Catholic so my mom would pay less for something she already could not afford.

I was baptized in a Christian Church, I don't remember the name of it, but while Thyl was in college at UM. She joined this Christian Church, and they were certain that the other churches had it wrong. The Baptists, the Protestants, the Lutherans, and the Catholics were all mistaken. The "one true church" was the "Christian Church" and even though I thought I had been baptized four times, none of them counted. I had to be baptized again in the "one true faith." So, I got baptized for the fifth and final time. After being baptized I was considered "saved," but something happened the following week that caused a chink in my Christian armor. One of the other students at Central heard me mention something about God. He asked me, "Are you one of those church kids?" "No," I snapped. Even though that was a minor instance in life, it brought to mind quickly when Simon Peter denied Christ. I felt like I had already failed in my journey towards Christendom.

Religion and my relationship with God was a circuitous journey for me. In addition to the five baptisms at one point after reading Malcolm X's Autobiography I was a declared atheist. I just couldn't quite wrap my mind around all the images of white Jesus and white angels and white Mother Mary at school and in my home and in some of the black churches I attended. Even though I wanted to be a policeman, I understood what Muhammad Ali and Malcolm X meant when they said that if you

An Intimate Conversation

shaved his hair and beard the images of Jesus they put forth would look just like the same white police officer beating black people's head in.

At a point in life Rony was my best friend. Rony had gotten saved in high school as well. One day, I shared with him that I was an atheist. He said, "You are, are you? Isn't blaspheming against the Holy Ghost the only unforgivable sin?" I did not know what "blaspheming" meant, but the term unforgivable frightened me. It was one thing to glibly say I was an atheist, but at that time I still had a very real belief in Hell. The possibility, however remote, of an eternity in Hell was too strong for me and from that moment forward I believed in God and prayed nearly every night that I could remember.

I will say that while I was an atheist, I felt an emptiness inside. Later I read some of the works of Saint Augustine where he said that we're all born with a God filled void. I can't say all because I don't know all people, but I can say I definitely felt that void when I chose to believe there was no God. I have not felt that void again since I let God back into my heart.

These days since 1989 I have been worshipping with then Pastor, now Bishop, Victor T. Curry.

Even though I grew up in Miami I did not find him, my wife found him when he was a pastor at Mount Carmel. I got married at Mount Carmel. Although Pastor Curry was the senior pastor, by then my brother Bobby was an ordained A.M.E. minister and he performed the ceremony.

Shortly, after we got married Bishop Curry left Mount Carmel to form his own church, and we followed him. We have been worshipping under his pastorship since then. I didn't bother to get baptized again. I think five times were enough. I did have both my boys christened and baptized by him, so for now they are still members of New Birth Baptist Church.

Q: Did anybody teach you how to fight in your life?
A: From kindergarten through Holy Redeemer, I was not a good fighter so I cannot really say that anybody taught me how to street fight. Being a boy, I did know how to wrestle, but I really didn't know how to throw a punch. So much so that one of the few punches I remember was punching my brother Chuck in the face. One of Chuck's favorite pastimes was bullying me. Once when we were living in the projects—don't ask me why I was wearing my Aunt Bern's clothes, but it tickled me pink to have on high heels and her little necklace, and a hat. I went outside and walked through a breezeway. As I

An Intimate Conversation

exited the back side of the breezeway, I felt some dirt thrown in my face and somebody beating me with a stick. I did not know who it was nor to this day do I know how my mother knew what Chuck had done; but when I tell you she beat him, she beat him. From then on he still made it a point to bully me. He was only thirteen months older, but much heavier, stronger and way more athletic than I was. One day in the above ground pool in our backyard, he was having his fun pushing me down shoving me around. I balled up my fist and hard as I could, I punched him in the face and then I ran in the house. He came in the house and wanted to fight me, but mom stopped him and asked us what happened. He told her that I had hit him in the face. I told her he had been bothering me, like he always did, so I hit him. She looked at Chuck and said, you probably were bothering him, which was the truth.

As a teenager, Thomas, the policeman that lived in the corner house on my block, spent some time teaching me Karate and Judo. I learned a few holds, kicks, and punches, but that is as far as it went.

An interesting thing happened after my growing in size and strength. Because I was bullied I despised bullies. Being the youngest of eleven but specifically of eight boys, I did get knocked around a bit by Isadore, Chick, and Chuck. I don't remember Noggie ever bullying me or putting his hands on me. As I got bigger and stronger in high school I felt like now I could handle any of them in a fight, but I had no desire to fight my brothers. Isadore had gone away to the Air Force and then come back from the Air Force I'm unclear why. He said he got a medical discharge because he had to have surgery on his lung, and he did have a scar on his chest, but I still don't know the particulars. Isadore was naturally strong, could fight, could draw, and was handsome. During basic training he was up to 225 pounds. Whatever happened after the surgery he lost about fifty pounds of that and then he came home. I guess going from being a strong teenager to an even stronger man in the service, but then losing all that strength was hard on his psyche. After a time, he wanted to build his strength back. He would see me in the backyard lifting weights every day. So, he eventually began to start lifting weights. Because he had not had to work for his strength, he lacked the discipline to train rigorously. Boys will be boys and even though Isadore was seven years older than I was, he challenged me to a wrestling match. Not only did I have him down within a few seconds, but I guess I grabbed him in such a way that I touched that surgical scar and he shrieked in pain. Now looking back on it I don't know if it was the pain of the scar or the humiliation of being overpowered by his younger brother. I don't care, which it was, I never laid hands on him again.

There is a little craziness in my family. For me growing up in the ghetto and being able to fight kind of went hand in hand. At least that was my reality. Looking back on it I realized it wasn't true because there were other people who grew up in the ghetto who never threw a punch and went on to do very great things in their life. When I raised my sons one of the things I told them was that I was a police officer and I was called to violent situations and in many times I had to use violence to bring people under control, but it didn't make me any better than my friend David, who was at that time a supervisory assistant state attorney. He had one of the most brilliant legal minds I ever came across, and I came across many. I told my sons; I was pretty sure David never came close to a fight in his life; yet he was a great and powerful man. He probably put more people in jail than most of the state attorneys in Miami-Dade County. I gave them the option that if they wanted to learn how to fight and be fighters that's fine but physical fighting isn't the only way to get through this life.

I do believe in owning a firearm, as I think it's important to be able to protect yourself, your home, and your family. I was a police officer for twenty-seven years and even before that I saw enough bad stuff happen to know that just hoping somebody will not hurt you doesn't guarantee they won't hurt you.

Q: Do you remember any concerts from your early life?
A: One of the concerts I remember is going to see the Spinners. Rony had a cousin named Kat. She was petite probably about five-feet tall, bowlegged, and positively gorgeous. I'm not sure why she agreed to go to the concert with me, but she did. By that time, I was driving so I got to drive her to the concert in my sister's brown Ford Torino. She was my date for one night. It did not go any further than that because she was taken and smitten with a young man named Cheever who went to school with her at Miami Carol City. She later married him, and they had two sons.

By the time I was fifteen I had put on weight to pass for eighteen. My sister Toy and I went to Shula's Night Club in Fort Lauderdale, were we saw Bobby Womack, one of my favorite performers. His songs *Harry Hippie* and *That's the Way I Feel About You,* must have played over and over in my mind more than a thousand times.

An Intimate Conversation

I remember going to see Luther Vandross in concert on three separate occasions. I like music as a space filler, but I don't have the passion for it like my wife does. She could listen to music all day. For the last decade or so she and I go to Miami Gardens annual Jazz in the Gardens concert, a two-day music festival featuring several artists. I enjoy parts of it: seeing old friends, and the tasty foods they sell. Now it's just a long two days for me. Also, with the advent of vaping, cigars, and things that are allowed in open air concerts, it's just not my vibe anymore. One year, my friend Da-Venya gave us tickets to go see Alicia Keys at the Hard Rock Café. That was more my jam, inside, air condition, no smoking, no weed, and a great sound system.

Q: What television shows did you watch growing up?
A: In elementary school and a little bit in high school I watched a lot of cartoons. Because I had a little talent for drawing I liked to watch the cartoons. Eventually I became captivated by police shows because I wanted to be a police officer like my brother Bobby. That's why I watched anything police. *Barnaby Jones, Cannon, One Adam-12, Dragnet, Tenafly*, and the list goes on.

Q: Have you ever been in a fight?

A: A few shoving matches, but the only real fight I had was with a kid named Keith. We got into an argument over a softball game, and he pushed me down and we scuffled a little bit. I didn't like the way it ended so the next day I saw him at the grocery store and really got into it with him. I won the fight easily. Years later Keith would get a black belt in Karate. Dummy me, I decided to challenge him to a sparring match. Not because I had taken Karate, but because by then I had a good twenty-five pounds on him. He was so good and so fast that I never saw the first few punches he threw. He told me he didn't want to spar, and that was A-Okay with me. I knew I was outmatched, but I also grew in my respect for him.

I must have been in the ninth grade, when I had a humiliating near-fight is how I would describe it. This kid named Pig was on our street, because he knew some of the other kids on the block. I don't even remember what started the whole thing, but he wanted to fight me. I wasn't that big, but I was bigger than he was, so I didn't want to fight him, but he kept egging me on. Each time I approached him, he'd back away. Dumbly, I turned my head to tell the onlookers, "See, he won't fight me." While my head was turned, he snuck up on me sucker punched me and took off running. I chased him and chased him, but I could never catch him. Somehow in the

An Intimate Conversation

street lore got recorded that I lost the fight. I saw him a couple of years later and I think he thought I still gave a darn about what happened. We were in a group of teenagers, and he kept angling away from me to try to get out of my reach. My brother Chuck, picked up on it and told me about it later. I told Chuck, I was done with the matter and had no interest in fighting somebody over something that happened two years ago.

Q: Who taught you how to drive?
A: I was taught to drive by several people. My brothers Chick and Noggie; Driver's Education in high school. Noggie's friend Cleve taught me how to drive a stick shift, which I can still to today.

Q: Do you have the same best friend from when you were younger?
A: Over the years I've had different best friends. For a time Juggie was my best friend, then Rony, then Reggie, and finally Irving Thomas who is my best friend to this day.

Reggie and I were best friends at Central, and something happened to him I won't share it because it's really his story not mine, but it damaged him and left him with an overwhelming sense of guilt. He was angling to be a doctor but ended up joining the Jehovah's Witnesses after he graduated high school.

I am not sure why joining a Church meant he had to quit college but quit he did.

Like my sister Thyl, he wanted me to become a part of the Jehovah Witness Church. Like my sister, he felt he had found the "one true faith." I wonder how many wars have been waged on that premise. When I rejected it he rejected me as a friend.

This was a repeat of my experience with my sister Thyl. She felt like the Christian Church she had joined had gotten it "all right" and the others had gotten it "all wrong." She believed mom and the rest of us were all going to Hell. She refused come to parties for the family and things like that. I remember mother saying to her, "If you're a Christian but you refuse to be around people who are not Christian how will you ever save anybody or help anybody not saved to get saved?" It was a cogent argument.

Q: Did you go to summer camp?
A: Upward Bound at Florida Memorial College if that counts. Not overnight camps, but summer programs at the University of Miami and at Miami-Dade.

Q: Have you ever gone camping?

An Intimate Conversation

A: As a kid the closest I went to camping was when I was an Explorer with the Miami Police Department. We took a field trip over to the Sebring for the Sebring 500 race and we slept in tents and ate breakfast in a common area. A more favorable memory was as an adult when I got to chaperone my son's field trip to sea camp down in Key West Florida. It was meant for the children, but I got to tell you it was the best field trip of my life. We slept in cabins; they would ring the triangle that lets you know it's time to eat. We would wake up to see deer walking around and waiting to be petted, and we got to swim with sand sharks and snorkel down to the reefs. It was awesome!

Q: Who do you remember encouraging you when you were growing up?
A: Thomas, the policeman on my street, Bishop William, our next door neighbor and landlord, and my sister Toy.

Q: Did you go on any family trips?
A: I don't remember any.

Q: Name one person that you helped when you were a kid?
A: The homeless man who lived in the alley behind Juggie's house. I scraped together enough money to buy a loaf of bread, which I gave to him.

Q: Who was the first person that you knew that died?
A: My uncle, Isadore "Uncle Doe," Aunt Bern's husband. I think it was a heart attack.

Q: Can you ride a bicycle?
A: Yes.

Q: Who taught you to ride a bike?
A: I don't remember for sure.

Q: Did you play any sports?
A: Briefly and weakly at Holy Redeemer, but after high school, I played for a neighborhood football team called the Opa-locka Crunch Bunch. A couple of things here was that I was bigger and stronger and also I was an offensive lineman, which meant I didn't have to handle the ball, just protect the offensive backfield. I played until one of the games degenerated into a fight and near gunplay.

Q: Where did you go to get your hair done as a kid?
A: Beck's Barber Shop. There was a barber their named John, who opened his own Barber Shop, and I began to go to him.

Q: Do you remember how old you were when you started growing a mustache?

An Intimate Conversation

A: I do not, but I don't remember having a moustache in high school.

Q: Do you remember the first person you ever had sex with?
A: I remember, but I want to protect her confidentiality.

Q: Do you remember the first date you ever went on?
A: I would say the time I took Mary to the Men of Tomorrow. It was a coming out event for high school juniors. I was a tenth grader, sophomore, but my brother Chuck was an eleventh grader. I was going to support him. I thought the date meant we were boyfriend and girlfriend, but the next week when I walked out to her school to see her; and see her I did, kissing another guy. Fortunately, Pearl, my sister Thyl's friend had warned me. Pearl went to Miami Northwestern and knew Mary. I didn't want to believe Pearl, but she was right.

Q: Who taught you how to shave?
A: I learned more by watching my older brothers rather than any one specifically teaching me. I remember Isadore and Ronald using Magic Shave. Magic Shave was a paste you put on your face, then scrapped it off with the dull end of a butter knife. I did this because I learned early on that I could not

use a razor, which caused me razor bumps. Magic Shave had a pungent order and if you left it on your skin too long, it would irritate the skin.

One day, I went to the barbershop with Lawrence, one of my high school classmates. He had a full beard in high school. He could not shave either, so the barber used T-Edger clippers to shave him. The electric edger did not cause razor bumps. When I started shaving, that is what I used and still use to this day.

Q: Name one thing you got in trouble for when you were in middle school?
A: Stealing from the Kash N' Karry.

Kash N' Karry
One afternoon we were coming back from a summer sports program at Miami-Dade Junior College. The bus put us off on 66th and NW 22nd Avenue. Frank, one of the older, stronger kids on my block dared me to steal a pint carton of Jungle Juice from the Kash N' Karry convenience store. He said he would steal one first. He went in the store while I waited around the side. When he rounded the corner of the store he had a Jungle Juice carton in his hand. I went in, stole one, and came out. When I came out Frank and the other kids burst into laughter because Frank had bamboozled me. He had

found an empty carton on the ground and acted as if he stole it. Even though I didn't get caught, my brother Chuck still told my mother. I cannot remember if she whipped me or not, but I do remember my brother Isadore being furious at me: not for stealing, but for being tricked into stealing. The stealing itself, he did not have a problem with, but that I was tricked was what upset him.

Q: One thing you got in trouble for when you were in high school?
A: Truancy in the tenth grade. Once I got to Miami Central, I was a reinvented student. I avoided trouble. In order to attend Central, which was in the school district north of the one I lived in, I had to use Charles' address. Charles was a friend of my brother Chick. Near as I can figure, Charles did not have a job and lived with (or off of) a nurse named Sandra, who had a son named Ricky. The lived in a two-bedroom duplex and my brother Chick lived in one of the rooms. If there were any notices, such as truancy, tardiness, or failing in classes the notices would go to Charles' address. I don't remember what he notice was for, but I know it was negative. One afternoon, I stopped by Charles' apartment, and he showed me the notice. I am not sure if he shared it with Chick or my mom, but the look of disappointment on his face made me disappointed with myself. That is the only negative

correspondence I remember receiving from Miami Central. From that point forward all that was sent was my report cards and they were all favorable. So much so, that in my senior year, I began making the principal's honor roll. I not only got my name mentioned on the school's public address system, but I also got to leave class to go to a reception held at the adjoining agricultural school. I was proud and to this day remember the red punch they served.

Q: Name one thing you got in trouble for when you were in college.
A: I got an "F" in Religion at Florida Memorial College. I stopped attending, because I planned to drop the class, but I missed the drop deadline. For the semester I attended Florida Memorial, I got three A's and one F. Instead of a 4.0, I got a 3.0. No matter, how much I appealed I could not get the F removed. That was a hard academic lesson that some mistakes can't be fixed. I even went to the professor's home, unannounced to ask if he would remove it. I figured since he was a reverend, asking forgiveness might work. It did not and he was incensed that I came to his home.

Q: Tell me about a random memory from middle school.
A: I was in the eighth grade and Remy was in the sixth grade. I had asked her to be my girlfriend, and

An Intimate Conversation

she said, "Yes." This really didn't mean much, because her mother did not allow her to date, but whenever possible, we stole phone calls in the evening. Back then the only phones were hardline phones in the house and the only time she could call was when her mother was in the other room. Still, to me Remy was beautiful: curly jet black hair, tanned skin, and what passed as a nice figure for a sixth grader. Imagine my heartbreak on the last day of school, when I saw Greg kissing her on the west side of Holy Redeemer. I was crushed and never called her again. One day after I had finished high school, she showed up at my house. I was perplexed and had no idea what she wanted from me. We sat for a few awkward moments and strained conversation. I think I told her that I saw her and Greg, but even years later, it hurt too much for me to even what to be friends with her.

Q: Do you remember your first kiss?
A: I was in a summer program at the University of Miami. I know Juggie was in the program with me, but I don't remember who else from 65th Street went. We would walk from 65th Street to Charles Drew Elementary where a nice, air-conditioned bus would pick us up. The bus would also pick up kids from other neighborhoods and by the time we got to UM, the bus was full. The bus chaperones, who looked like adults to me, I realize now were

university students with summer jobs. I know this because my sister, Thyl, was at the UM, and knew one of the chaperones. As college students, they were about two years removed from being high school kids themselves. Mostly they sat in front of the bus and as long as the students weren't killing each other, they let them be. A girl from one of the other pickups, sat next to me on the bus. She told me there was another girl in the back of the bus that wanted to teach me how to kiss. I looked back there and older girl, by that a mean a high school girl, beckoned me with her finger to come back there. She was a heavyset, pretty girl wearing sunglasses. I didn't want to seem scared, even though I was scared. I went back there. That was how I learned to "French kiss." It was nice!

Q: Have you ever gone horseback riding?
A: I have. After graduating high school, I found a riding ranch in North Miami and went horseback riding. No one ever taught me, but the ranch hands were knowledgeable, and it was a leisurely ride through a tree-lined trail. I think when I started dating my wife, one of our dates was to go horseback riding.

Q: Did you like college?
A: I was not familiar with the term "imposter syndrome," but I would say that my first semester

of college which was at Florida Memorial, and then definitely my next few semesters in Miami-Dade Junior College I suffered from imposter syndrome. Being sneaky like I could be, I realized that I did not have to take the Scholastic Aptitude Test to go to Miami-Dade come so I went to Miami-Dade College at which was at that time a two-year Community College. I started out going to Florida Memorial, and I was on financial aid, but even with that I still came out owing them $185. They would not release my grades until I paid the $185, which I had to do in order to transfer over to Miami-Dade. When you attended Miami-Dade you got financial aid which at that time was a BEOG basic education opportunity grant which I got because in short we were poor. I had heard my brother Kelsey managed to finagle away to be registered in Miami-Dade under two different Social Security numbers and collect two different financial aid checks. And as soon as he got the checks he would withdraw. The checks would pay for the classes but there was an overage of $700. He would just cash the checks then withdraw from his classes. Sounded like a great plan to me so I did the same thing. I got away with it for two semesters before they put me on academic probation. At which time I stopped attending Miami-Dade. I had in my mind that I was going to build a landscaping empire. So, I bought some lawn mowers, and a 1958 Chevy pickup and started cutting yards. Initially I work with some guys on my block that I grew up with, but I realized I was doing the most work and they would come in and help but they had other jobs and other commitments. I ended up messing up a friendship trying to do business with friends, specifically with Anthony. I don't know if I ever apologized to him but basically he was working another job and they would come and work with me catches catch can, and finally I just told him no I'll just take over the whole business. If you don't know what you want to do in life blistering your hands while working in the hot sun and dealing with equipment breaking down will help clarify it for you. That being said once I realized I was not going to build a big landscaping business, I have to thank my cousin Walter Junior for giving me a job at Quik Mart. I did not know it at the time, but that job would carry me for the next six years. While working at Quik Mart I still did yards on the side, but I got back in school and went to Miami-Dade, with renewed vigor.

When I told my brother Ronald that I was going back to school he asked me, "Why?" Let me back up; before that when I told him I was dropping out of college, he said, "Chances are you won't go back." When I told him I was going to go back he asked, "Why?" He said going to school for school sake doesn't make any sense and chances are you're not going to finish. Let me say with all the affection I can muster I love my brother dearly, but boy did I want to gut punch him for that. Nevertheless, it was the kick in the groin I needed because I did not only get back in, and finish Miami-Dade I actually made the Dean's list for the last two semesters I was there and won a small scholarship to continue my education at University of Miami. I also need to thank Walt and Vern. Walt because he hired me and Vern at Quik Mart. After Walt left and Vern became the manager, the entire time I was in college Vern kept me on at the store. Also, he left me on the books as fulltime, which gave me sick leave, vacation time, and health insurance. More than that, I was able to keep a little money in my pocket and keep my car on the road.

Q: Did you ever win any awards in college?
A: Yes, I returned college after my probationary period had expired. I met a young man name Lee, who became an inspiration for me.

Lee
Lee was majoring in computer sciences, but he worked fulltime had his own apartment and car and still made straight A's. He showed me that it could be done. Although I wasn't working full time, and I had a car off and on depending on whether or not the car worked, I really poured myself into my

studies. One of things that I started doing was as soon as I got an assignment rather than go home I went straight to the library and did the assignment. Therefore, for the last two semesters of Miami-Dade I made the honor roll and impressed the professor in charge of the business department. When I told him I was going to visit my brother in Chicago for the summer, he arranged for me to have an interview for an internship at Price Waterhouse which was one of the big eight accounting firms in the nation at that time. I did not get a job or internship, but I did end up getting a Price Waterhouse scholarship for $1,000 which helped with text book costs when I finished Miami-Dade and went to University of Miami.

Students in Free Enterprise
Unrelated to my academic career, while I was at Miami-Dade was the only time I ever voted Republican. I was in a model course called S.I.F.E. Students in Free Enterprise, that was designed to teach us how to be entrepreneurs. The instructor was a guy named Steve who had Republican leanings and convinced me that Reagan knew what was best for the country. Another thing that Steve did for me help me deal with my anxiety about going to UM. I didn't think I was up to the task so Steve said if I would come by his house he would work with me tutoring me in accounting. And I did

go a couple times, and he did tutor me. I also went on a one week fast thinking that it would clear my mind before I got to UM.

Prior to attending the University of Miami my grades were scattered. Sometimes high, sometimes low, but I recognized that the grades reflected the amount of work I put into the course. Most of the classes I took if I had really applied myself I was able to understand them. I figured I was going to major in accounting because that seemed like the best way to make money, even though I did not like accounting. To make things worse, Intermediate Accounting was the first class I took that I genuinely try to pass and could not get it. I went to the instructors, I spent hours in the library, there were just concepts that I could not get. Later, Ronald told me that one of the things about studying business that he learned in college is that many of the concepts were abstractions for him. Whereas for many of his white counterparts whose parents or other family members actually owned businesses they were not abstractions they were actual practicable tenets that they had seen applied. Ironically, even though I didn't get a good grade in accounting, I actually tutored a lady named Jackie and accounting and she managed to not only finish accounting but get a degree in accounting and went on to work for Bank of America. I also tutored a young lady whose father owned a liquor store up in New York, this was in computers back when computers were first starting up. I remember she paid me $50.00 to tutor her and I also remember she drove a sports car called a Lancia. I told my Italian roommate Tom that the lady drove a Lancia. Pronouncing it *lan-see-a*. He said if you go into a car dealer and pronounce it that way they're going to charge you an extra $5,000. My roommate was Italian and owned a sports car. Again, abstraction versus concreteness.

I did not win any awards while attending UM. I worked a sixteen-hour shift at Quik Mart on Saturdays. Quik Mart was forty-mile round trip drive in Miami traffic. By doing all my hours in one day, I only had to make the drive once a week. I got through my year at UM with five A's, two B's, and one Withdrawal. My financial aid wasn't enough to cover it, so I ended up having to borrow $3,500.00. Back then, that was about one-third of the value of the house my mother lived in. By the end of the semester, I just couldn't stand being broke and in debt anymore. I didn't think I was going to finish my degree, and I did not like business, I was not enjoying the fact that I had racked up $3,500 worth of debt.

Chicago

An Intimate Conversation

When the school year was over, for the second time I went up to Chicago to visit with my brother Ronald. I was supposed to get a job at the post office as a summer temp. However, when I went to the orientation one of the things they told me was that if someone stops you at the corner and orders you to give them the mail don't fight them give them the mail. What they plan to do is take the monthly government checks from the people who live on the block and then have the people pay them to give them their checks. Upon hearing that and also hearing a lot about the number of gangs that existed in Chicago I quickly decided that was not a job for me. This was 1982, when unemployment was at a record high in America, while Ronald Reagan was president. Specifically, one of the cities with the highest unemployment was Rockford, Illinois, which was eighty-six miles east of Chicago. In Chicago, a department store was set to open and was taking applications. Twenty-five hundred people showed up to apply. Oblivious to the dour economic outlook surrounding me, I donned a nice pair of trousers, a pressed shirt, and the tie. I got on 1-90W, drove south, and took the Exit to Calumet City. When I got off, I saw a Quik Mart store on my left. I had left Quik Mart on good terms as I had worked very hard and never missed a day the entire time I was in college.

I walked in the store and asked the young lady hey are you looking to hire anybody. She looked at me and my necktie and starched shirt and said we are, but I don't think we pay enough for you because we start out at minimum wage. I told her that's not a problem because I already worked for Quik mart for five years in Florida. They'd probably start me where I left off. She called her district manager, who called Tom, the district manager in Miami. Tom said he wished he had ten more like me. I was hired immediately.

Nevertheless, she was suspicious of me, which I did not understand but later came to understand it. One day she asked me was I a plant sent by the company, and I said no, which was true I was not. I thought it was a strange question. It turns out she was stealing and thought that the company had sent me there to catch her. Because she had the brain of a gerbil she was caught stealing and fired and her number Two was put in charge of the store. Thaddeus, well-dressed tall Greek guy with olive skin met me and I impressed him with my work ethic and neatness. He asked me if I would like to manage a store out in Addison, which was in a suburb thirty-three miles west of Chicago. I took the job and confirmed what I already suspected. I was not returning to UM. A store manager's job did not pay a lot, but it was

An Intimate Conversation

more money than I had ever made, and I was not racking up any more student loan debts.

While in Chicago I was living with my brother Ronald. I told him I did not plan to return to UM, and he said, "Let's see how it plays out." I worked my heart out and actually turned the store around very well. One of my funny memories was when a young black lady came in and said she was looking for a job and asked to speak to the manager. I told her I was the manager, and she said stop playing around, then left without filling out an application.

I also met a seventeen-year-old named John. The other employees described him as a troubled youth who had been banned from the store. When he came in one day, my assistant manager had warned me not to let him in the store because he had been caught stealing. Since, have been caught stealing when I was younger I didn't consider that unforgivable. When he came in the store, I introduced myself as the new manager. He grabbed a pack of gum and as he paid for it, he said, "You know I'm banned from here from stealing." I said, "As long as you don't steal anything else, you can come back." He didn't steal anything else, and we became friends. I was a few years older than he was, so it was more a mentor / mentee relationship. I eventually came back to Miami, and John went on to join the army.

I remember my last day at the store, one of my employee's wife had baked me a loaf of banana nut bread to take on the drive. It was the first time I remember having banana nut bread and I've liked it ever since.

Q: Name one thing you got in trouble for when you were in college?
A: The one thing I got in trouble for was receiving my BEOG (Basic Education Opportunity Grants) overage checks and then withdrawing from classes. That's what got me put on academic probation.

Q: Can you describe a fond memory from college?
A: When I returned to Miami-Dade College after cutting yards for a year, physical education was a requirement. I took ballet and racquetball. I enjoyed them both and for a moment I thought maybe I could do ballet. I did get an A in the beginning class, but then I went to an audition for the advanced class. I watched this white kid who happened to be in there just loosening up. Another young lady was auditioning, and her dance partner did not show up. I watch the white guy learn our routine in fifteen minutes and execute it flawlessly. I knew right then that those students had been dancing way longer

An Intimate Conversation

than I had and I didn't stand the chance, so I opted to discontinue ballet. I will say one of the pleasant parts of it was when we were getting dressed for performances the ladies were not shy and taking off their leotards and showing their G strings. I rather like that part of it. Coincidentally I did date one of the dancers named Layla. I don't know where she's living or what she's doing now and if she wants that part of her story told. She could have been a professional ballet dancer: lithe, supple, fluid and could do a full split. She was a Muslim and told me she didn't eat pork. At the time I said that's no big deal I'm a vegetarian, which was shocking to her because she said when she told most black people she didn't eat pork they were not understanding of that. One of the nicer things she did with me was making me a vegetarian dinner and had me watch a show called *Hill Street Blues*. It was a police show set in a city made to look like Chicago. And the main character was Captain Frank Furillo, who was a recovering alcoholic. A couple of things happened there one being that I remembered how badly I wanted to become a police officer, and something about him being a recovering alcoholic resonated with me. Layla and I did not last. She was in the U.S. Army Reserves. I am not sure what happened, but we just decided it wasn't going to work and when our separate ways.

Q: Were you in the armed forces?
A: I was not in the armed forces. I missed the armed forces on two counts. Three if you count the Coast Guard. One count was that President Nixon had ceased the draft right before I was due to sign up.. The other thing is there was an obscure law on the books I don't know if it still is, but I believe it was on the books then. If a mother had children in every branch of the service then she didn't have to let one of the other children go. Bobby had been in the Army, Sonny had been in the Navy, Chick and Isadore had been in the Air Force; Noggie had been in the Marines. Every branch was covered. After I finished high school and was floundering around deciding what I wanted to do I had ran into a Coast Guard recruiter. I talked to my friends Rony and Roger about what the guy had said. None of us had any idea what we planned to do as a career. So, we all went and took the test. At the time the Coast Guard had had something called the buddy system where if you joined you would go to the same assignment. I passed the entrance exam, but Rony and Roger failed. If I enlisted, I would have had to go it alone. I chickened out. Later, I learned the Coast Guard did not fall under the Department of Defense rather it fell under the Department of Transportation. Somehow, it counted as civil service and if you went there you didn't have to go in any other branch in the military.

An Intimate Conversation

Q: Who taught you how to tie a tie?
A: I think Chick taught me how to tie a tie. I know he taught me the difference in a Windsor knot and a half knot.

Q: How old were you when you got your driver's license?
A: In Florida you can get your learner's permit (restricted license) when you're fifteen. This allows you to drive a car as long as there is an adult in the passenger seat next to you. I got mine on my fifteenth birthday, and when I turned sixteen, I got my operator's license on my birthday.

"No means no!"
On my sixteenth birthday, I skipped school, borrowed my sister Toy's car and Joi, a white girl that I was dating at the time, also skipped school, and came with me that day. I passed the driver's license with no problem and then drove out to my Aunt Bern's house, because I knew she would be at work, but I knew how to get in the house without a key. I planned to have sex with Joi that day, unprotected sex which may have ended badly. We did a lot of kissing and fondling, but she said "No," on sex. Later, she ended up dating another African American student and confessed to me that she had gotten pregnant for him and had to have an abortion.

One good thing about sexual conduct that I learned early on is that "No means no!" When she said no, I did not force her. It had to be something we both wanted, not just me. Also, I probably had the IQ of a gnat when it came to sex because I didn't even understand condoms or how to use them.

Q: Who took you to get your driver's license?
A: I drove myself to get the driver's license and lied to the examiner and told him my sister brought me.

Q: Did you ever have any pets? If you had pets? What kind of pets did you have? What were their names? What happened to them?
A: I had a couple of stray dogs growing up. Crossbreeds mostly. And then Sage who I thought was a German shepherd but was really just a little crossbreed mutt.

Q: Were you ever seriously ill as a child?
A: The only time I had to go to the hospital was for nosebleeds. But I never broke or injured or anything severe enough to have to be hospitalized for it.

Q: What do you remember about your college graduation?
A: What I remember about my college graduation from Miami-Dade Junior College was how proud I was. I did not graduate from UM and chose not to

march when I finished high school. When it came to going to Miami-Dade College, nobody forced me to go or to go back and finish, but I did. My gown was light blue; the graduation was held and the stadium at Miami-Dade. My mother, my sister Toy, and my brother Big Bobby were there. Lois and Laverne were sisters, and both were on staff at Miami-Dade. Lois used to date my brother Chick and had known me since I was fourteen. She and Lavern helped me immeasurably and immensely to get myself unscrewed. I would not have gotten my degree without them. Coincidentally, they were at the graduation because their mother, Ruth, had decided to go back to college as an adult and their mother and I graduated in the same class. That day I went to Wong's Chinese Restaurant with Lois and her mom, and my mom and I forgot who else, and I remember I paid the entire bill for everybody's food at the Chinese restaurant. I knew of the restaurant, because when I told Lee I was a vegetarian, he took me there and ordered me a vegetarian dish. To this day when I think about my graduation my heart swells with pride. Bobby gave me a card with an Arabic Proverb in it that I still remember:

Men are four:

He who knows not and knows not he knows not; he is a fool - shun him;

He who knows not and knows he knows not; he is simple - teach him;

He who knows and knows not he knows, he is a sleep - wake him;

He who knows and knows he knows; he is wise - follow him."

Graduating the Police Academy
At my graduation from the Police Academy, I was ecstatic. I wanted to be a police officer since I was five, and this was my dream come true. I asked my brother Bobby who had been a police officer and my inspiration to do it to give me my badge. You are allowed to do that when you have a family member that's a police officer, but he couldn't make it that day. Instead, my nephew Little Bobby who was the City of Miami police officer gave me my badge. Kim and I were not dating anymore but she was in the same class and graduated as well. Her mother and father were there. My fondest memory was my brother Noggie in the back of the gym. He screamed so loud when they called my name, I could not help but smile. I will always remember that Noggie was an awesome cheerleader for those he loved.

An Intimate Conversation

Q: Would you rather be the oldest child or the youngest child in a family?
A: As I am the youngest child in the family I'm okay with it. My best friend, Irving, is seven years younger than I am. My mom met Irving and told me part of that friendship was because I was missing something in my life. She suspected I was missing that I never had a younger brother. Maybe I would have been okay as an older or oldest brother.

Q: If you could choose one of three superpowers, to the invisible, the breathe underwater, or to be able to fly, which would you choose?
A: I would want to be able to fly hands down. Because you can just go wherever you want when you want it. And the other superpowers you are limited geographically to where you can use them.

Q: Are there any songs that make you sad when you hear them?
A: Before I got sober, that is, before I stopped drinking completely, a lot of songs made me sad. I grew up during a time when music videos were first starting on television. A lot of music videos made me sad because there were always these beautiful people having great times and living great lives and I just felt like my life paled in comparison to that and that used to make me sad. A specific song that makes me sad is: *It's so Hard to Say Goodbye to*

Yesterday. I enjoy movies and for a time when they used to be on videotapes my nephew Bobby taught me how to copy them and so we had a bunch of copied videos. Then the film industry switched to DVD's. At one point I had maybe 700 DVD's in alphabetical order and that was even after giving away 50 to 100 a year. Either way I like movies I like going to the movies as a kid and especially watching movies at home with my sister Toy. To his day I still watch a lot of movies. That particular song *It's so Hard to Say Goodbye to Yesterday* was the closing song to a movie called *Cooley High.* The movie spun a coming of age tale about two high school friends in Chicago. It had all the things that came with high school: athletes, book worms, first kisses, and fights. In the end, the end the main character was beat to death by these two neighborhood hooligans. I cried, and to this day the song saddens me. Another song that moved me was *Rainy Days and Mondays,* by The Carpenters. My prom date and girlfriend at the time, Ava, was extremely beautiful and sang soprano. For her senior talent show, she sang that song, as I sat in the audience in love for the first time in my life.

Q: Are there any songs that make you happy when you hear them?
A: *Ti Amo* and *The Impossible Dream* from *Man of La Mancha.*

An Intimate Conversation

Q: Did any movies ever make you cry?
A: *Cooley High*.

Q: What books did you read if any and what are some of those you like better?
A: I've probably read more than 1,000 books in my life. For a time, *The Godfather* by Mario Puzo was one of my favorites I may have read it four times. Two of my current favorites are *The Alchemist* by Paulo Coelho; then *Of Mice and Men* by John Steinbeck.

Q: Have you met any famous people in your life? Who and how?
A: I met Muhammad Ali two times. The first time was when he opened a restaurant on 62nd Street and 17th Avenue called Champ Burger. There was a mob to get in there the first day and he was actually at the store letting people in the door. I met him again when he was doing a book tour here in Miami and my wife, Kim, a police officer at the time, was assigned to him for security.

Q: Do you own a firearm?
A: I own several firearms. I don't own any rifles anymore. When I was younger one of my recurring nightmares was somebody holding my wrist, overpowering me, and being so strong that no

matter how I fought I could not get away from them. When I turned eighteen I went to Woolco and purchased me a double barrel shotgun with buckshot loads. From the time I had that gun I never had another nightmare about being overpowered. Later, I bought a Mossberg pump shotgun, then later still, I bought me a Taurus .38 caliber six shot. The Taurus I used to keep in the store when I worked for Quik Mart. First, I kept the shotgun, but my cousin Walt left it in the store one weekend and it got stolen. Once I became a police officer the gun I was assigned was a Ruger .38 caliber which I still have. When we went to semiautomatics, I bought me a Smith and Wesson 5906, later we went to Glocks, so I have a Glock. My wife was also a police officer she went from a Ruger .38 to a Beretta 9 mm fifteen-shot. I have a collection of guns that my older brother Harold had before he passed away.

Q: Do you like plays?
A: I have only been to a few plays. When I went on the trip to Washington DC in high school we went to see this gospel play called *Your Arms are Too Short to Box With God*. I saw *Dream Girls* in Chicago with Kim's mother and father, when Kim and I first started dating. My best memory of a play, was *Ain't Misbehavin'* featuring Nell Carter. I saw it at the Coconut Grove Playhouse with my first

love Ava. To this day I hop on YouTube and rewatch it.

Q: Do you like speaking in public?
A: I do like speaking in public. I have spoken over the years and as I said in high school when I got to be the master of ceremony for the Miss Miami Central pageant, I enjoyed it. I've spoken publicly at my church. I delivered my grandniece Tosca's eulogy after she committed suicide. As a school resource officer, I taught (D.A.R.E.) Drug Abuse Resistance Education to fifth and sixth graders. Since I've retired I teach Struggle Well for the Boulder Crest Foundation which is a strategy to help first responders deal with trauma. I'm also vetted by the, Department of State to teach certain anti-terrorism courses to include Hostage Negotiation, First Response to Terrorist Incidents, and Managing Major Criminal Investigations.

Q: When were you married?
A: I was married May 26th, 1990, at Mount Carmel Baptist Church. Victor Curry was the pastor at the time, but my brother was also a pastor at a different church. We got married at Mount Carmel because it was our home church, but my brother Bobby performed the ceremony.

Q: Who was there?

A: As far as who was there, the guest list numbered over 200 people. Who wasn't there was my brother Chuck, my sister Thyl, and my sister Betty. The other brothers and sisters that did come were in the wedding. On Kim's side of the family quite a few people came in addition to her immediate family, her grandmothers were there, her paternal grandfather, countless cousins, and other relatives. Also, some people that I knew and did not invite showed up and said they knew I meant to invite them. They were right and I was glad to see them. I had warned the caterer that might happen and told him just bill me for any extras, which he happily did.

Q: Who was your best man and maid of honor?
A: I had two best men and there's a story behind that. One of my best men was Irving my best friend and without saying he was going to be my best man. The other person I asked to be my best man was Thomas, the police officer who mentored me when I was growing up. What I did not know was there was stress between him and my brother Bobby from back when they were both police officers and once he knew Bobby was performing the ceremony he didn't want to do it. That being said I went back to Rony who had been my childhood best friend and asked him to be the best man. Kim's two maids of

honor were her sister Sherri and her best friend Cynthia.

Q: Were you ever a best man?
A: I was indeed the best man at Isadore's wedding which was strange to me because I thought he and Noggie were closer than he and I were. It probably was because Noggie used to date the woman that Isadore married and it would have been awkward. Either way I was happy to do it. Then I was the best man in James' wedding. James was a dear friend and one of the associate pastors at my church.

Q: Where was your wedding reception?
A: A funny memory from our wedding day was that the chauffeur who drove us from the church to the reception was an older guy who seemed to be having trouble seeing. On top of that it was raining that evening. It was an exciting ride back then, but now it is a laughable recollection. The reception was in a hall over in Hialeah somewhere.

Q: What color was your tux / gown?
A: My tuxedo was dove gray, Kim's gown was white, and the bridesmaids colors were lavender.

Q: Who gave the bride away?
A: Kim's father Tyrone Senior gave her away.

Q: Who was the ring bearer?
A: The ring bearer was Kim's nephew Marcus who was Sherri's son who was born when I had visited Chicago.

Q: Who was the flower girl?
A: The flower girl was my grandniece, Tirzah's daughter, Rayna.

Q: Do you have children? What are their names and birthdays?
A: I have two wonderful sons. Joshua Laurick Ingram born August 3rd, and Jawanza Kevin Harold Ingram, born November 27th.

Q: How many nieces and nephews do you have?
A: I have so many nieces and nephews that if I give a number I will probably miss one or more of them. Currently, we have family members spanning four generations. That means I have nieces and nephews; my nieces and nephews have children; and my nieces and nephews' children have children. So, I have great grand nieces and nephews.

Q: How many of your cousins can you name?
A: Again, I come from a big family and they're eleven of us, then there's my mother's brothers and sisters, and my father's brothers and sisters, ergo, more cousins than I can count. Some that I spent the

most time it would be Walter Junior, and Wilbur, Junior. Wilbur makes it a point to keep in contact with this side of the family. Then there is Yolandi, who is not a cousin by birth but is close and is a member of New Birth Baptist Church where Kim and I worship..

Q: Who are you close to in life?
A: I am closest to my best friend Irving, my wife and children, my brother Ronald, and Da-Venya.

Q: Are there any nieces or nephews you are particularly close to?
A: I am particularly close to most of my nieces, nephews, and their children. Bobby's two daughters are Tirzah and Tammy. I am close to all the Tirzah's girls: as well as Tammy's daughter and son. I'm close to most of my brothers' children. My sister Thyl has ten children, but I don't really know them nor have a relationship with them because Thyl does not talk with me as of the writing of this book. My sister, Betty, had four children Robert (Little Bobby), Estherlina, Chris, and Tyke. I know them but was closest to Robert. For a time, he and I were roommates and both police officers. He worked for the City of Miami, and I worked for Miami-Dade County. I talk to Estherlina and was fond of her, but I would not call us close.

Q: Have you ever gone skydiving?
A: I have never gone skydiving. I did train to skydive, but I never did it.

Q: Did your life turn out like you expected?
A: The part of my life that turned out like I expected was becoming a police officer. I wanted to do it from when I was a small child and God blessed me to be able to do it for twenty-seven successful years. When I left the Police Department my desire was to be a bestselling author and travel the world, that did not turn out the way I wanted. Also, I wanted to be able to build a business that was self-sustaining and could be handed down to my sons, I have built businesses but they're not self-sustaining in the sense that if I'm not there the business goes away. However, it is not over until it is over, and I am still working on that legacy enterprise.

Q: What did you expect?
A: See the previous question.

Q: What didn't you expect?
A: Because I was a successful police officer, detective, and Sergeant I assumed I could take those skills and transplant them into other fields and would be equally successful. Others tell me I have done that, but I don't feel like I've done it or

An Intimate Conversation

succeeded at the level and the goals that I wanted to succeed.

Q: Is there anybody that you would like to apologize to? Even if you do not know them?
A: They're not a lot of people I want to apologize too because my plan for living involves apologizing when I'm wrong or if somebody says I'm wrong even if I don't see it I'll apologize. I don't really have a large inventory of apologies to be made. Miss Barbara from Miami Central. I went to the front office to complain about her being a little too friendly, and I think I was dead wrong I think she was just being friendly. I'm going to get back to this one because there are some things I'm sure are still vexing me today that I've not been able to go back in make right.

Q: You have a favorite outfit, or can you describe one of your favorite outfits?
A: I do not really have a favorite outfit which is odd considering my father was a tailor and my mother was a seamstress. Because I was such a fan of Muhammad Ali and Muhammad Ali generally just wore black suits or white shirt and a tie. Otherwise, he were khakis and a polo. Once I left the Police Department, I largely wear jeans comfortable shoes and Polo-type shirts. I do have a couple of Guayabera shirts that I really like. But I don't have

a suit that just makes me wish I could wear it all the time.

Q: What was your biggest financial setback?
A: I had a big reversal in the stock market I was up quite a bit for the year, and my plan was once I was up to sell off in September and lock in my profits and I didn't and then it was a big downturn, so I ended up losing all of my profits for that year. Actually, it's worse than that and I lost not just my profits, but I lost the profits on both accounts my account and my wife's account. Oddly enough I've made a lot of money in my life and a lot of successful business ventures, real estate, the job has done me well, walked away with a lot of money on other deals, but that loss just really hit me hard.

Q: What was your biggest financial success?
A: My biggest financial success was being a police officer and having the job. It paid very well it allowed me to have excellent insurance buy several houses take good care of my children and take all kinds of trips. Since I left the next biggest success was the sale of our primary residence we made a nice little sum on that, and we sold it at the top of the market. It was amazing we put it on the market on Saturday, and it was sold by Monday morning at 11:00 for our asking price. I also had a couple of

condos that I bought at tax deeds and almost double the price. One of them tripled in price.

Q: Have you ever had your heart broken?
A: I did, I did, starting with Ava. I don't think she meant to break my heart, but when Ava went away to college, I just knew that she was going to find somebody smarter and way more successful than I was. So, my stupidity said instead of waiting it out I would break up with her and that way she wouldn't be able to break up with me. That was a bad call.

Q: Have you ever broken someone's heart?
A: As far as whether or not I broke somebody else's heart I don't know if I'm equipped to answer that. I think they would have to answer it. There was a young lady I dated named Beverly, and I don't think I treated her as I should have. I don't think I cared for her as much as she cared for me, and I knew that, but I continued to date her. I broke up with her and 1 year later, stopped by her dorm in Tennessee to apologize.

Q: What is your favorite ice cream?
A: My favorite ice cream comes and goes. I like cherry vanilla, but at different times in my life I liked butter pecan, but currently vanilla bean is near the top. I will say my favorite brand is Haagen Daz.

Q: Do you like carnivals?
A: I don't like carnivals so much because I don't go on carnival rides so much. Growing up in South Florida the Dade County Youth Fair was a big event and I did enjoy going to it but at this stage of my life I go more for the food and to watch the younger kids enjoy themselves. I will say thanks to Saint James A.M.E. Church, I got to go to Disney World the first year it opened in Florida, and I've gone there maybe fifteen or twenty times if I include when I took my own children. I can honestly say, I never had a bad time at Disney. Even though I'm not a big roller coaster guy Space Mountain is the only roller coaster I like.

Q: Do you have any phobias or things that give you the creeps?
A: I had a phobia, but I don't want to put it in writing because I was delivered from it mentally and spiritually and I don't want to give it any more power. I wouldn't call it a phobia, but tree frogs creep me out.

Q: Do you like to fly in airplanes on trips?
A: I do prefer to fly; especially when going long distances, I would much rather fly than drive. Before I got sober I used to get anxious on flights and would drink before I got on the flight and hoped that I would be sleepy and sleep through the flight.

An Intimate Conversation

Now, flying doesn't bother me. I have done a couple of flights as long as twenty-three hours. Not all at once but on a four-leg flight I was on a plane for twenty-three hours over the course of two days and it didn't bother me. I enjoyed the food, the movies, and I slept. I do require an aisle seat. Very hard to be in between somebody or pressed against the window on that long flight.

Q: Do you like the zoo?
A: I could take her leave the zoo.

Q: Did you have any pets?
A: As an adult the only pets I had were fish and once my sons said they wanted a dog. I got them two small turtles. I told them if they could take care of the turtles then I would consider getting them a dog. They did not take care of the turtles, so we never got a dog or cat. Definitely not a cat because Kim's allergic to cats.

Q: Do you like dancing?
A: Sometimes I like dancing. In college I wanted to be a better dancer and I also felt like I needed an aesthetic component to my personality. Since I couldn't paint—I could sketch but not to a level that I liked. I decided I would take ballet to give myself an aesthetic dimension to my personality. I did

enjoy it when I took it. Now a little bit of line dancing is what I do most.

Q: Do you like singing?
A: I like songs, but I don't think I really have a great singing voice so not so much. I do sing along a lot of times when I'm in the car by myself.

Q: Can you draw?
A: I can draw but not great and I say that because I compare myself to my brother Isadore who could do masterful things with a pencil; and my brother Ronald who could sketch rooms when he was an interior decorator. I can sketch okay, but nothing to write home about.

Q: Do you like cooking?
A: I can cook, and I cook more when the boys were in elementary and high school than I do now in retirement. I cook about once a week. Mostly I eat out.

Q: What is your favorite food?
A: I don't have a favorite food, but I probably eat steak more than anything else, prime rib and rib eye being my preferred ones. I do like sweets, so I have to watch that.

Q: Do you have a best friend now?

An Intimate Conversation

A: My best friend since 1982 has been Irving Thomas. And he is still my best friend.

Q: What is your wedding anniversary date?
A: My wedding anniversary date is May 26th, 1990.

Q: Were you ever in the hospital?
A: To date I've never spent the night in the hospital. I've gone to the hospital for sickness and injuries. I've injured myself and got knocked out at work once. I also had a bad sciatica flare up, but I never spent the night in a hospital.

Q: What is your dream job?
A: My dream job would be to be a bestselling author and traveling the world sharing my books that entertain educate and edify the people who read them.

Q: Do you have a favorite movie?
A: I don't have a favorite movie. I have a cluster of movies that I like. *The Godfather* with Marlon Brando. *Claudine* with Diane Carroll and James Earl Jones. The original *Sparkle* with Irene Cara. When I was younger I thought that I was going to grow to be famous and rich and marry Irene Cara. I never even got within a hundred miles of Irene Cara.

Q: Can you play a musical instrument?

A: I do not know how to play any instruments other than chopsticks on the piano. I toyed with the harmonica for a minute, but I don't even know how to play one of those.

Q: Are you in any clubs?
A: I am not in any clubs nor fraternities; I'm not a Mason; I'm not an Elk, or anything like that.

The Fraternity Thing
I didn't do the fraternity thing for two reasons: One is I didn't like the fact that if I joined I was in it for life and could never get out. The other thing is I made a mistake when I saw something and let that thing define fraternities for me. While I was attending Florida Memorial College, a guy named Joe was pledging a fraternity, I don't remember which one. I admired Joe because Joe was there to get his degree even though he had a bad stutter when he spoke. I thought about the courage it took to go after his degree with that speech impediment. Anyway, he was pledging, and I don't know what his Big Brother or whatever told him to do but I saw the Big Brother chastise him and then slap him. Having grown up in a house of fighting brothers I resolved that nobody was going to be putting their hands on me. So, fraternities were off the table for me. That is a classic error of inductive reasoning where I took one thing and applied to an entire idea

or concept. These days, I have nothing against fraternities or sororities. My wife is a proud member of Delta Sigma Theta Sorority Incorporated. My brother Chuck is Sigma and Big Bobby was a Kappa and a Mason.

Q: Do you have any tattoos?
A: I do not have any tattoos. Again, things I can't undo worry me and tattoos fall into that category. When I was growing up one of the big things was to get gold teeth. Many of the kids up and down the street had gold teeth which was curious considering we were in the ghetto, and they were spending money on something they probably could not afford. I asked my mom if I could get one she said absolutely not and she wouldn't even discuss it.

The one thing she didn't mind me doing when I was fourteen was piercing my ear in fact she pierced my ear for me, and I wore an earring for a short time but that was not long lived.

Q: Who taught you how to cook one dish?
A: I learned how to cook from various people, but who taught me the most about cooking was my sister Toy. To this day I remember that cabbage is a weeping vegetable, and you don't need to use water to cook it. *"I love and miss you, sis."*

Q: What is your favorite dinner?
A: I don't know if this counts as a favorite but in Florida I enjoy when stone crabs are in season. Traditionally for Father's Day I go to the Rustic Inn Crab House and have a big plate of Dungeness crabs. I guess a favorite would be the surf and turf at Benihana the steak and scallops on the hibachi along with pork fried rice.

Q: What food do you eat the most?
A: I eat fruit and drink milk daily.

Q: Do you have a favorite dessert?
A: Again, like with the ice cream Haagen Daz would be my brand of ice cream, I don't really have a favorite dessert I like a lot of desserts.

Q: Do you like cold weather?
A: I do not like cold weather which is why I live in South Florida. I lived in Chicago for one year and it was brutal for me. I did not like shoveling snow I did not like icy roads, and I did not like having to wear layers of clothing. Usually for Christmas I'm wearing jeans and a polo, because that's Christmas in South Florida.

Q: Do you like the beach?

An Intimate Conversation

A: I like the beach, but I don't go there as often as I used to. When I go I usually just sit in the water now whereas I used to go and swim.

Q: Which of the four seasons do you like better?
A: Again, winter in Florida could be 72°, I'm only going to say winter because Christmas falls during the winter, and Christmas is my favorite holiday.

Q: Have you ever been in a fight?
A: I have been in fights as a kid I've already told the story about Pig and about Keith. As a police officer I got into fights arresting people.

Q: Do you like your body?
A: I do like my body but growing up I admired bodybuilders, and I had hoped that I would be one of those older guys who was ripped and well defined, but I'm not. I'm in decent shape I work out three days a week and go to the gym, but I'm not really cut or shredded the way I would like to be. I'm still working on it.

Q: Do you watch professional sports?
A: I rarely watch professional sports including the Super Bowl and the NBA Finals. My wife is actually a bigger basketball fan than I am. And although my best friend was a professional basketball player and I followed him religiously

when he played, I just don't really watch professional sports that much. In my younger days because Muhammad Ali is on my list of ten people I admire, I followed boxing while he was fighting. Once he stopped, I watched it intermittently, but no other champ captivated me like he did.

Q: Do you remember where you were when Martin Luther King was killed?
A: I was home because I remember my mom screaming and crying Oh my God they killed him they killed him.

Q: Can you recall a fun memory from college?
A: The thing that comes to mind I will not share because of course it involves a young lady, and I want to respect her privacy. Other fun things included making the Dean's list my last two semesters and graduating from Miami-Dade College.

Q: Were you ever a victim of a crime?
A: Yes I was robbed at gunpoint twice when I used to run convenience stores. I've also had a couple of my cars burglarized.

Q: Did you ever commit a crime?
A: A few in my younger years. I already mentioned the time I stole Jungle Juice from Kash N' Karry.

An Intimate Conversation

Also, for shoplifting at a store called JM Fields on 27th Avenue 167th Street. I learned a good lesson from the incident at JM Fields. I am not sure it matters, but Roger was Frank's brother. The same Frank that snookered me into stealing a Jungle Juice.

You Never Have to Steal
I went with my friend Roger and Juggie and we agreed to go in the store and steal something. I was going to steal a leather steering wheel cover to give it to my sister Toy. I did not hear Roger say that if anybody gets caught don't come back. Roger got caught an+ d I went back and turned myself in. It wasn't until later that Juggie told me what Roger had said. I guess Roger expected me to get caught not him. Either way I was processed, that is, technically arrested and given a promise to appear. I was released and allowed to go home. When I got home, my mother already knew and was furious. My brother Isadore said I was stupid for getting caught. Toy was heartbroken. Of everything that happened, hurting Toy was what I felt the worst about. She told me that you know all you had to do was ask me and I would have bought you whatever you wanted. You never have to steal. Toy's comments cut me to the quick. For a couple of weeks after that, every chance my mother got she would berate me telling me, "If you lie, you'll steal and I hate a thief!" This

confused me on a couple of levels. First, I knew my mother to lie quite a bit. Moreover, I knew her to have stolen money that other family members had hidden around the house. Finally, I guess I had heard it one too many times and I lashed back. I said, "Mom, premarital sex is a sin, but you did it and that's how you got pregnant with Bobby!" My brother Chuck was in earshot of us, and he came onto the porch, grabbed me by my collar, and shoved me down. He asked me who I thought I was talking to. I didn't fight him back, but mother never said that to me again.

Another inconsistency about Chuck was that he was the one who told on me when I stole from Kash N' Karry. He was the one who roughed me up for talking back to mom. Then one day somebody stole two of his hubcaps off of his Pontiac. He came and got me and asked me to go steal two from somebody else for him. Like Boo Boo the Fool, I did it and got away with it. Maybe Isadore was right: "I was stupid."

Q: What feature do you like most about yourself?
A: The feature I like most about myself is my mind. If it's a physical feature it would probably be my arms.

An Intimate Conversation

Q: What bodily feature would you like to change about yourself?
A: The feature I would like to change most is to have a smaller waist. It was tapered when I was younger and as I've gotten older it's been harder and harder to keep it tapered. Hard, muscular, but not tapered.

Q: Knowing what you know today what advice would you have given yourself in the first ten years of your life?
A: Knowing what I know today the advice I would have given myself in my first ten years of life is the same advice I gave my sons. Even when people mean well and give you advice, investigate experiment, challenge, and prove for yourself whether it is good advice for you. A lieutenant over the bomb squad once told me, "There's a lot to be said for great training, but experience is the best training." I would tell my ten-year-old self to be careful, be honest but be courageous and don't be afraid of experiencing things for yourself.

Q: As a teenager?
A: As a teenager I would have told myself that having unprotected sex with young ladies that you don't really have a deep feeling for is not a good start. Take your time, get to know the person, allow the person to get to know you, and if you decide to

have sex, have protected sex until you're ready to have a child.

Q: Do you have a Bible verse you like?
A: James 1:19 (NKJV) "Be swift to hear slow to speak, slow to wrath..."

Q: What jobs have you had in your life?
A: I've had a lot of jobs.

Race Didn't Seem to Matter
The jobs that stand out were the earliest ones I had, which was emptying the trash at Holy Redeemer after school. Helping Bishop William cut yards during the summer. Working at Quik Mart, which I started in 1979 and stayed there until I finished college and got hired by the Police Department in 1985. Then the twenty-seven years of honorable service of the Miami-Dade Police Department; truly one of the great experiences of my life. Another job that I remember was in college I went to work for UPS during the Christmas rush. The work was grueling; we had to unload tractor trailers. What you would do is you would started the tractor trailer which was filled to the back door. We're talking about a fifty-foot trailer filled from floor to ceiling. And then one by one you take a box put it on a wheelie track and roll it down to the conveyor belt you were expected to do 1,500 packages an hour. It

was backbreaking work. I ended up getting fired. I won't go into why, but I'll tell you it was my fault. I'll also say that I felt like I disappointed one of the supervisors there. He was a white guy from Mississippi who could not pronounce my name to save his life. He kept calling me Laverick, but he did his best to move me out of the trucks, get me into different positions, and try to get me on as a permanent person. Basically, I self-destructed on that one, but it's one of the instances in my life where race didn't seem to matter and how well I was treated. I don't remember his name, but I am grateful for what he tried to do for me.

Q: What is the first raise you ever got if you can remember?
A: Working at Quik Mart, after six months or something like that, my cousin Walter who was the manager gave me a $0.50 an hour raise. Then when I got on the Police Department and would get my annual reports, they came with nice raises.

Q: The first time you ever got promoted on the job?
A: My first promotion was at Quik Mart, when I was promoted to store manager. Dean Thaddeus, the district manager for Chicago, asked me if I wanted to run the Addison store and promoted me to manager.

Q: Do you speak any other languages?
A: Spanish.

Q: Do you carry any pictures around with you?
A: I'm going to answer the question because I still carry a wallet, but I don't know how valid it is in this day and time. I carry one picture in my wallet. It's a picture of Josh and Jawanza when Josh was at Phil's Academy and Jawanza had not begun school yet. I had trouble getting Jawanza to sit still for a picture and what I decided to do was on the day that they were doing school pictures for Josh, I dressed Jawanza up and brought him with me. I had the photographer take Josh's individual picture and then asked him to take a picture with Josh holding Jawanza. Jawanza finally sat still for that picture. I had it laminated, and I carried in my wallet. The reason I say I don't know how valid that is anymore is because that predated cellphones where you could walk around with 2,800 pictures in your pocket or on your belt.

Q: Do you carry a wallet?
A: I do still carry a wallet. And I also carry my badge case with my retiree badge and my credentials for private investigation and firearms qualifications etcetera.

Q: What do you have in your wallet right now?

An Intimate Conversation

A: I usually have extra cash at least $100 tucked away, my driver's license, credit cards, and my health insurance cards.

Q: Have you ever broken any bones?
A: I have never broken any bones. I have strained muscles and dislocated my wrists. I've also hurt my back, but I've never broken any bones.

Q: Have you ever been in any car crashes?
A: Yes, I was in a car crash when I was small, and my sister Betty was driving. As I recall it was near 22nd Avenue and Alibaba. I remember my mom hitting her head and having to take stitches across her forehead and I remember biting through my tongue and my tongue bleeding.

Q: Who taught you how to kiss?
A: I already shared the story about riding the bus from University of Miami and the young lady teaching me how to kiss.

Q: Anything you remember about your wedding day?
A: I remember many things about my wedding day. But one thing I remember is prior to the ceremony I walked across the street to the Amoco gas station and bought myself a can of Pepsi. I stood out there, and I drank the pop and asked myself if I wanted to

go through with it. And the answer was, "Yes," so I walked back across the street and married Kim.

Q: Where did you spend your honeymoon?
A: We had three different hotel rooms. The first one was over on Miami Beach, and then my godmother gave us a hotel room over by the airport with a seven-hundred gallon tub in the center of the floor, and then finally the full honeymoon was in Naples, Florida, and we stayed at the Registry Resort with a view of the Gulf of Mexico. Coincidentally, in 2025, I celebrated my thirty-fifth wedding anniversary and did a vow renewal ceremony on the beach in Nassau, Bahamas.

Q: Do you have any children about which you don't talk?
A: No, I talked about both of my sons.

Q: Do you dream a lot when you sleep?
A: I do dream a lot. I don't put a lot of stock in dreams which has to do with one time I dreamed some numbers, and I went to the dog track and played them in twelve consecutive races. I ended up losing $1,100 in one night. Considering it took me a year to save $1,500, that was a hit. Also, other than $2.00 on a lottery ticket, here and there, I don't gamble anymore.

An Intimate Conversation

Q: Do you remember your dreams?
A: I do remember my dreams, but I don't keep a dream journal.

Q: What restaurant do you go to the most?
A: I don't know if it counts as a restaurant, but I go to Starbucks twice a day. When I lived down in Pembroke Pines I would go to Sergio's Cuban Restaurant twice a day. The Cuban restaurants in Port Saint Lucie don't have the quality of Cuban coffee this Sergio's has. Also, a lot of the staff and Sergio knows me, and I feel very comfortable being there.

Q: What do you order when you go to that restaurant?
A: Cuban coffee.

Q: Have you ever won any awards for anything?
A: I have won awards. I won a second place writing award in the eighth grade for an essay on being *Young, Gifted, and Black*. As a police officer I had somewhere north of one-hundred commendations for things ranging from public speaking to life saving events and special campaigns like when the Pope came to visit Miami. When I retired I got several awards from the different federal agencies I worked with, Federal Bureau of Investigation, Secret Service, Bureau of Alcohol Tobacco and

Firearms, and the US Marshall's Office. On the Police Department I won Officer of the Year for a big narcotics case that my partner Brownie and I did.

Q: What fruits do you like?
A: Oranges and bananas.

Q: Do you wear glasses?
A: I wear glasses now. In my forties I was still working on the job and reading police reports and then one day I noticed that even though I was signing off the different boxes I couldn't see the fine print in the boxes. The other thing I noticed was whenever I would go out to dinner I would have to use my phone's flashlight to read the menu. Eventually I succumbed and bought some cheaters. I started out with a 150 magnification. At the time of this writing, I'm at a 300 magnification. The glasses are worn for reading. I don't wear glasses while driving as I have no issues with farsightedness. Nor do I have any issues with night vision.

Q: Is there anybody you would like to say you are sorry to?
A: My high school classmate, Lawrence. When we were in Upward Bound we would ride the bus out to Florida Memorial College for the summer

program. One day we were coming back on the bus, and it was me and Lawrence and Angela. Some hooligans in the back of the bus were trying to make a move on Angela even though she was sitting next to Lawrence. Lawrence and Angela were not boyfriend and girlfriend, but Lawrence was sweet on her. Nevertheless, the crew in the back of the bus was rude and rowdy. Lawrence actually knew one of them. So, they began arguing and I was trying to tell Lawrence don't argue because we were outnumbered but probably because Angela was there he didn't want to seem like he was afraid, so he kept arguing with them. When our stop came and it was time to get off I walked to the front of the bus, but Lawrence decided to get off on the back of the bus and as he did one of the guys reached over and punched him in the head and he now went back in the bus to fight them. When I saw them attack him honestly my legs almost froze I was so afraid. I saw some police officers and I walked over to the police officers I didn't run I walked, because I was terrified. I told them what was happening, so the officer saw it. He and his partner ran back to the bus at which time Lawrence came out of the bus and was bleeding from a scar below his eye which never fully healed. The first thing he shouted to me was, "Where were you?" Angela later told me that she saw me walking over to the police; not running to them. It was a moment of cowardice on my part, and it broke my friendship with Lawrence. I did actually apologize to him and told him if I had a chance to do it again, I would not have left him. He told me, "If ifs and buts were candy and nuts, it would be Christmas all the time," which meant he didn't accept my apology. From then on, he was anxious to see me fall on my face any place or anywhere. Later in life he committed suicide, for reasons I will never know. I did talk to him once or twice after we were adults. He phoned me once on a police matter night and helped him where I could. "Lawrence, I say again, I'm sorry I failed you as a friend."

Q: Is there anybody you believe owes you an apology?
A: That's a tricky one I'm going to say probably one of them is my brother, but I don't want to say which brother because in the event that his children's children read this I don't want to make a record of wrongs. My mother dealt with a lot of resentments and a lot of hurt for things that were done to her in her early years, and she brought them up quite often. One of her pet phrases was, "I'll never forgive [fill in the blank] for what he / she did." I didn't want to bring that into this generation. One of my brothers was an Olympic class liar. He was several years older than I was. Once he dropped mother and I off at the Northside Shopping Center. He was supposed to come back and pick us up, but after two hours

mother figured he wasn't coming back and we walked home. Later, that evening he came to the house and when mother asked him why he hadn't come back like he said he would, he told her he had come back. I shouted, "You're lying!" At which time, he grabbed me and flung me across the kitchen. I was hurt on two levels. First off, he was lying. Next, mom knew he was lying and did not take up for me.

I was grown with children when I finally realized my brother was an alcoholic and mom was afraid of him. I did not think my mom feared anything, but I was wrong. Having had my own challenges with drinking and now being sober thirty-six years, I have been around enough alcoholics and addicts to know that many of them lack the capacity admit when they are wrong. Ironically, mother was not an alcoholic and rarely if ever admitted she was wrong—so, fruit, tree. Add to that that my dad let that brother get away with anything he wanted, and it makes sense, he would not feel like he owed anyone an apology. He used to say, "If the world doesn't owe you anything, then you don't owe the world *shit!*" I never expected, nor ever got an apology for the many—and I mean many—times he wronged me.

Q: Do you prefer showers or baths?

A: I prefer showers to baths even though we have two tubs in the house, but I like the walk-in shower with the double nozzles.

Q: Do you have a favorite artist? Art could be sculpture, painting, or whatever you define as art.
A: I don't really have a favorite artist in terms of painting or sculpture or things like that. Obviously, I have songs that I like more than others, but even then you know I guess Luther Vandross would be one of the artists that I actually went to see the most of any other person.

Q: Do you like clothes and dressing up?
A: I used to like dressing up, because my brother Chick was a clothes horse and my brother Ronald also was very meticulous about his dress as was big Bobby. I stopped caring about it when I read Muhammad Ali's biography and when I met Muhammad Ali. Mainly because Muhammad Ali used to wear khakis and a pullover most of the time, unless he was wearing his black suit and tie if he was going to the mosque or appearing on television. At that point I really became very relaxed in my attire, like today I probably own more jeans than anything else. So, my usual attire is jeans sneakers or soft shoes and a Polo shirt. In 2025 I did start buying clothes and shoes again so I'm back into it

but nowhere near like my brother Chick who would match down to his underwear.

Q: Do you like hats?
A: I rarely wear hats.

Q: Name a commercial that made you laugh?
A: There are a few that made me laugh but there's an old Super Bowl commercial, Terry Tate Office Linebacker "Super Bowl Spot." It is a spoof where they hire a professional linebacker to keep the office in order. It just tickles me to this day whenever I see it. And the other one is the most interesting man in the world when he used to advertise for Dos XX beer.

Q: Do you have a piece of jewelry that is important to you?
A: The pieces of jewelry that were important to me I have given to my sons leaving me with the only piece that's very important to me now, which is my wedding ring. I wanted the pieces was a cross that Toy gave me, the other is the hand of God my friend Suzy gave me; finally, a cat eye ring that my brother Sonny gave me.

Q: Do you have a favorite team in sports?
A: I do have favorite teams and for me it's all things Florida. The Miami Dolphins—God help me—the

Marlins, the Florida Panthers, and now we have a soccer team. If we get a WNBA team, I will support them as well.

Q: Do you have any hobbies?
A: If binge watching Netflix counts then that would be one, and the other would be listening to audio books.

Q: Have you ever been arrested?
A: Technically arrested when I was fifteen for shoplifting, but it was a non-custodial arrest. That's where they fill out the arrest form, release you on your promise to appear in court at a later date.

Q: What type of weather do you prefer?
A: I lived in Chicago for a year and do not like snow or cold weather. I like sunny weather.

Q: Do you like holidays? If so which holidays do you like and why?
A: I like Christmas. I like the months of November and December. I like that time of year. I love the music, family getting together giving gifts and getting gifts. I also have the memories that even though we were poor because of mother, I never had a sad Christmas.

An Intimate Conversation

Q: Of all the cars you own which one did you like the most?
A: Out of all the cars I owned the one I liked the most was my 1979 midnight blue Cadillac Seville. Second to that was my 1987 Chevrolet Camaro IROC-Z (International Race of Champions) that I ordered directly from the dealer.

Q: Do you prefer sunrises or sunsets?
A: I prefer sunrises because they signal the beginning of a new day and another opportunity.

Q: Have you ever gone skiing?
A: I have gone neither snow skiing nor water skiing.

Q: Have you ever gone scuba diving?
A: I have not gone scuba diving, but I do know how to snorkel.

Q: Do you like boating?
A: I like boating when I go for example to go fishing on a charter boat or go out with my friend BJ and Mia on their boat. But I can take it or leave it.

Q: Have you ever ridden on, or do you know how to ride a motorcycle?
A: I do know how to ride a motorcycle I have ridden on motorcycles. I don't really care for motorcycles.

Q: Have you ever gone hunting or do you like hunting?
A: I have not gone hunting unless you count when I was a kid and we used to hunt pigeons with a BB gun.

Q: Name somebody you consider attractive and why?
A: Because I'm smarter than I used to be that's an easy answer my wife, because she's beautiful.

Q: Do you consider yourself attractive or handsome and why?
A: I do consider myself handsome, not Playboy-type attractive, but I think God dealt me a good hand to live life with. I'm tall, dark, healthy, and have been told I have a nice smile.

Q: What was the best vacation you ever went on and why?
A: Vacations plural the best vacations I've gone on are Paris, France, when I flew over there to be with my best friend Irving; Dunns River Falls, Jamaica; and Paradise Island, Bahamas, with Kim and the boys. We were over there for the wedding of her cousin Diane to Victor. It was a great vacation.

Q: Last time you did something kind for somebody?

A: I helped the young lady that was arrested in a case of mistaken identity. My son, Joshua, asked my wife and I to look into the case, my wife and I are private investigators. The young lady had been dealing with this case for more than two years. She had exhausted her savings hiring two different attorneys and she was no closer to getting the case dismissed. We took on the case *pro bono*. I have done over a thousand investigations. I warned my son not to be disappointed if I found out she may not have been telling him the truth. I was wrong, she was telling him the truth. Someone had stolen her identity and committed fraud under her name. Despite glaring flaws in the case, including an alibi witness, and pictures of the subjects that clearly were not her, she was still arrested and charged. We helped her get the case dismissed and get her life back. At least that part of her life.

Q: When was the last time somebody did something kind for you?
A: My neighbor across the street got the gentlemen who were pressure cleaning the sidewalks to pressure clean my sidewalk for me.

Q: If you were an animal, what animal would you be?
A: I would be in an American bald eagle. So, I could fly, live on high, and hunt from afar.

Q: If you could go back in time or forward in time which would you choose and what would you do once you were there?
A: I don't know if I can answer that. If I were to go back in time and have the knowledge that I currently have, it would be an awesome responsibility not to look things up. Going forward in time I would miss so much of the journey and how I got to where I got to. I will chalk that one up as an unanswerable question for me.

Q: List three values you consider important and why?
A: Growth which encompasses continuous learning, health, and wealth.

Q: When was the last time you cried?
A: I don't remember the last time I cried.

Q: When was the last time you laughed?
A: I usually find something to laugh about every day.

Q: When you wake in the morning what do you usually think about?
A: When I wake up in the morning I'm usually thinking about how grateful I am to wake up in the morning. Then I get dressed and quietly leave the

An Intimate Conversation

house to go get my coffee. En route to get my coffee I listen to audio books. Once I get my coffee, I play games on my phone to keep my mind sharp. After that I watch stupid YouTube shorts just for entertainment. Each time I go on my computer I view the verse of the day on Bible Gateway.

Q: When you go to sleep at night what do you usually think about?
A: At night I go down on my knees and thank the Lord for another day. I've been doing that since I was fourteen years old. I started out praying as a child. Except for the brief time that I was an atheist; I have prayed every night before going to sleep.

Q: How did you meet your wife, partner, significant other?
A: October 1983, I was at my brother Isadore's house, with a couple of friends, watching a boxing match. I did not really care about the preliminary bouts prior to the big fight, so I volunteered to do a liquor run. I headed off to the liquor store on Ali Baba and 22nd Avenue. While there, I ran into Sharon, who was dating a guy named Hamp, that worked for Vern at Quik Mart. Sharon said she had heard I was back. Sharon and some friends had been playing cards, so she had done a liquor run for her crew. I invited her out to see my Cadillac Seville that I had recently bought. While we were in the

parking lot, her friend Kim, overheard me say that I had come back from Chicago earlier in the year. She said, "I'm from Chicago." Then she asked me how I liked it. I told her I did not like it so much. She seemed incredulous that I would not find her city enchanting. Although I did not find Chicago enchanting I did find her attractive. As she and Sharon were returning to Sharon's car, I grabbed a legal pad from the front seat of my car, walked over to the door, where I asked her for her name and phone number. Later she joked that she was suspicious when I asked her for her last name because she was from Chicago and that was not something you shared with guys you just met. Keep in mind this was October 1983, before Facebook, Instagram, cellphones, TikTok, and the multiple ways that you could now look into somebody else's life. I did call her, and we did go on a date. The rest is history.

Q: What historical events have you witnessed that changed the way you see the world or left a lasting imprint on you?
A: They are:

- 9-1-1 attacks on the World Trade Center

- Martin Luther King Jr.'s Assassination

An Intimate Conversation

- JFK's Assassination

- Muhammad Ali's refusal to be drafted into the armed forces.

- Malcom X's Assassination

- Obama being elected president.

- Kamala Harris being elected vice-president and then running for president.

- The Space Shuttle Discovery exploding midflight.

- OJ Simpson being found not guilty (I believe he did it.)

- Jesse Jackson running for president. (One of his campaign stops was my brother Dr. Ingram's house)

- My brother, Dr. Ingram, when he was the Mayor of Opa-locka, welcoming President Mandela, when other Miami politicians snubbed him, because he refused to denounce Fidel Castro.

- The Bush – Gore election, when it was decided by a handful of voters in South Florida.

- The January 6th Insurrection in the Capitol when Trump lawfully and legally lost the election but refused to concede. This seemed to echo when the Union Army won the Civil War, and Confederate sympathizers refusing to accept the defeat shot and killed the president. In my life I have seen people who believe the rules only apply when they are winning. The January 6th Insurrection manifests that.

- The Christian "Right" willingness to adjust, rather ignore the things they purported to support, and vote for Donald Trump.

- Nelson Mandela being elected president after serving twenty-seven years in prison.

- The 5,000 Role Models founded by the Honorable Frederica Wilson with the help of my brother, Dr. Ingram.

- The COVID pandemic. The horror of it and the way it divided the country when I thought it would cause us to coalesce as a people.

An Intimate Conversation

Q: What personal tragedies radically affected your life outlook?
A: They are;
- The deaths of my family members, particularly, my mother and my sister, Toy.

- Detectives Roger Castillo and Amanda Haworth being murdered while working for me.

- Losing six figures in the stock market after I had retired.

- The times I got my heart broken.

Q: What personal triumphs radically effected your outlook on life?
A: The personal triumphs that affected my outlook on life are:
- Graduating from Miami-Dade College.

- Becoming a police officer; police detective; police sergeant, and hostage negotiator.

- Being able to travel and teach in other countries under the aegis of the Department of State.

- Going door-to-door for the Obama for President Campaign.

- Taking care of my older brother Sonny until he passed away from Alzheimer's Disease.

- Getting married.

- Becoming a father.

- Delivering my grandniece, Tosca's Eulogy.

- Keeping my promise to my brother Sonny that for as long as I was alive he would be in his house. He lived there until his final days.

- When I went to visit my sister Toy in the hospital, she was in a bad way. As soon as she saw me, she blurted out, "I'm sorry!" I had no idea what she was talking about, but I told her she had nothing to be sorry for. She was the best sister I could have hoped for. I also told her that I had had a vision earlier that day. While driving east on Pembroke Road, I looked up into the sky, and I saw our mother, Sister Marie, and Aunt Josephine (all of them had already passed away) seated on clouds and wearing white dresses. They told me to tell you that they were waiting for you. I also told her that she and I used to say that we would follow each other into Hell, but I no longer wanted that. Heaven is where she was going, and I would see her again someday.

Q: Can you name a famous person you admire?
A: In his book *Think and Grow Rich*, Napoleon Hill extols the value of having a "master mind" group. Essentially, a collection of people to help you develop and polish the ideas that will make you rich. In one chapter he explains how he would hold council in his imagination with ten men whose lives and life works had impressed him. I liked the idea of having a list of people whose lives and life works impressed me. To that end, I drafted two lists. One of famous or historical people and the other of people I actually knew. Here are my Top Ten from each category.

In category of the famous people my lists includes Muhammad Ali, Maya Angelo, King David, Leonardo Da Vinci, Hugh Hefner, Rudyard Kipling, President John F Kennedy, South African President Nelson Rolihlahla Mandela, William Shakespeare, and Bill W., the founder of Alcoholics Anonymous.

The reasons I admire them are as follows:

- Muhammad Ali for his prowess in the boxing ring but also for his stance for social justice outside the ring. And for his courage to embrace Islam during the time when even black people thought Islam was an evil threat to Christianity.

- Maya Angelou for the things she overcame as told in her in her book *I Know Why the Caged Bird Sings*.

- King David for his life's journey from shepherd boy to King.

- Leonardo Da Vinci, for his multifaceted genius in art, engineering, as well as words. His collected journals contained between 20,000 and 28,000 pages of notes and sketches. One of his contemporaries said he was strong enough to bend a horseshoe with his bare hands.

- Hugh Hefner for launching *Playboy Magazine*, which grew into a multi-million-dollar, multi-national corporation. More than that, for his courage to give a platform for people to speak who were firestorms of controversy in the 60's and 70's. I remember his magazine publishing interviews of Fidel Castro, Muhammad Ali, Malcolm X, Martin Luther King Junior. I also remember a time when he had a TV show and Aretha Franklin was scheduled to appear. Sponsors threatened to boycott him for allowing a black woman to perform on a syndicated television show. He told him go ahead but she still sings, and he allowed her to perform.

- U.S. President John Fitzgerald Kennedy because he was born into wealth and privilege but still lived the life that made a difference. He joined the military, he confronted the civil rights issues head on, and he was in chronic back pain but still campaigned and worked tirelessly to make the country better.

- Rudyard Kipling, for his prolific penning of poems, such as: *If, I Keep Six Honest Serving Men, Mandalay*; and his novel *The Jungle Book*, even the animated Disney version.

- South African President Nelson Rolihlahla Mandela for his tireless efforts of ensuring the rights of the majority of Black South Africans to vote and govern as opposed to being governed by the minority of White South Africans. President Mandela went into prison when he was in his forties when he came out he was nearly seventy. At seventy years old he ran for and successfully became the first Black President of South Africa. When I consider his twenty-seven years in prison many years of which were at the brutal Robben Island Prison, I think about how many times he could have thrown in the towel. Had he thrown in the towel, history would have been deprived of one of the greatest champions of justice to ever live. He's an inspiration at times when I feel like I can't go on and a reminder that it's not over until it's over.

- William Shakespeare for his incredible literary skills. I'm a fan of the written word and I'm a fan of the drama he could evoke with the artistry of his words. Also, his courage in 1604, to write Othello casting a North African Moor as the good guy, even though Shakespeare was English.

- Bill W., the founder of Alcoholics Anonymous. My life is better and fuller because of a man I never knew but a man who took the time to work with Alcoholics and write the Big Book with his original core group. I shudder to think of what my life would have been like if it were not for A.A.

Ten People I Know and Admire
They are Bishop Victor T. Curry, Rafael Fernandez, Craig Glover, Harold Ingraham, Arena Ingram, Arimentha Ingram, Robert Ingram, Ronald Ingram, Irving Thomas, and Tosca Marie Johnson.

- Bishop Victor T. Curry for his faith and vision to leave a church where he was established and

An Intimate Conversation

build a church from the ground up, which is New Birth Baptist Church Cathedral of Faith International. I'm not a founding member but was there when it was founded and have been there ever since.

- Rafael "Ralph" Fernandez, who was a Lieutenant on our Police Department. I was offered a job with the Recording Industry Association of America, because of a million-dollar piracy case I did for them. I turned it down but told them he might be who they were looking for. He interviewed and they hired him on the spot. Since that time, he's done extraordinary things from going to the Grammys to meeting with dignitaries all around the world. He's brilliant he speaks Spanish and English; he built a model Porsche in his garage and whenever he takes it out people give him compliments and want to take pictures by it. I think he's been married three times but somehow he maintains a great relationship with all his children from all his marriages. I just think he's brilliant and lives life to its fullest.

- Craig Glover and his wife Bonnie were friends of ours and their two sons Matthew and Ben are contemporaries of my two sons Joshua and Jawanza. Craig had a big financial reversal in life and additionally his wife suffered from kidney failure and was on dialysis. He was not a match for her once she got on the kidney transplant list, but he became part of an eight-way kidney swap to ensure that she got another kidney. Sadly, eight years after the transplant, Bonnie contracted COVID and died. Even after his financial reversal, he bounced back and tried his hand at three businesses and on the third, which was a home health care business, he hit a home run. The business occupies two buildings now and is growing from one city to another city. He's in great physical condition, he's passionate, he loves his sons, and he's a good friend.

- Harold Ingraham was my oldest brother, and he volunteered to join the Navy in 1943, during World War II. While in the Navy, even though he was a qualified quartermaster, because he was black once he graduated basic training they made him a cook. Nevertheless, he traveled the world with the Navy and then when he came back he went to work for Pan Am where he worked for thirty-seven years. He divorced once, but his second wife, Birdia, was the love of his life. He was an excellent role model for me as a husband. He taught me how to maintain my cars, he paid his bills in advance, he was physically strong. He was the embodiment of many things that a man should be, and he loved me.

An Intimate Conversation

- Arena "Toy" Ingram, my sister taught me the power of unconditional love. She loved me, bought me a ten-speed bike, and gave me my first car, a Ford Torino. Toy took care of me, and I enjoyed taking care of Toy. I used to work at a gas station, and she was still working midnights at the post office. While she slept during the day I would take her car and get it washed and gassed up. She loved movies and so I developed a passion for movies because I used to love to watch movies with her. She liked Vincent Price, who starred in horror films, and was the voice over for Michael Jackkson's hit song *Thriller*. She also liked to read what they used to call the variety pages and knew the back stories on many of the actors and actresses. To this day I still watch the Cary Grant movies which she turned me on to those along with William Powell movies. She was quite simply the best sister I could have asked for.

- My mother, Arimentha Ingram, makes this list. My mother was 5'5" tall and to the best of my knowledge did not have more than a fifth grade education. Nevertheless, she gave birth to nine children that survived and three that did not survive. She was also a step mother to dad's children from his "first wife," Rhoda Mae Hudson. She did beat us with a belt and sometimes with her hands, but I have no problem with this. I understand that might be argumentative in this day and time, but my mom was doing her best to keep young black boys out of jail and out of trouble and that's the way she did it. What I admire most about my mother was her ability to soldier on despite soul crushing setbacks and poverty. I have now been a father and a husband and understand some of the responsibilities involved. Unlike her, I had a good job, I went to college, my kids always had health insurance, we took family vacations. She couldn't provide any of that. What she did provide was to teach me how to work and most importantly to teach me how to read. She read quite a bit even though she didn't go far in school and she passed that on to me. She is one of the most courageous people I've ever met, and I don't know if I had been dealt the same hand that she was dealt that I would have made it. *Love you, ma!*

- Robert "Bobby" Ingram was my mother's first born and my father's third child. Bobby dropped out of high school but eventually went into the Army where he got his General Education Development (GED) degree, the equivalent of a high school diploma. He tells a funny story about how another army guy in basic training was going to the movies and asked Bobby if he wanted to go. Bobby said sure why not, and the guy said well I got to make a stop before we go. Since Bobby had nothing better to do, he went with the guy in the stop was for the guy to take his GED exam. Since Bobby was with him, he took the exam as well and passed. After he got out of the Army, he applied to the Miami Police Department. His godfather was one of the five black original officers on the department. Bobby was hired in 1959, the year I was born. Bobby touched my life in so many ways and was my inspiration for becoming a police officer. Once when I was five, and we were still living in The Projects, he came to visit mom In his police car. When he got ready to leave I asked him to turn on his overhead light. At that time, it was a single red bubble on top of the car's roof. He activated the rotating light, and it lit up the whole neighborhood. I knew at that moment I wanted to be a police officer. Twenty-one years later, I would end up wearing the silver badge. Beyond that Bobby was a force of nature. After he got on the Police Department he went back to college. While he was married with two children, he earned an associate's degree, a bachelor's degree a master's degree and a doctorate. He left the City of Miami as a Sergeant, went on to Opa-locka to be a Chief, and left there to be a City Manager of South Miami. He left South Miami and campaigned to be the Mayor of Opa-locka. Not only did he win the election, but he also won it multiple times. He resigned as Mayor to serve on the Dade County School Board. While serving as a School Board

Member, he was ordained as an African Methodist Episcopal Minister. While doing both those things, he was also a Professor at Florida Memorial University, formerly, Florida Memorial College. When he passed away there were more than 1,500 mourners at his funeral. The other thing big Bobby taught me was never stop learning. It was rare you saw him without a book or a notebook in his hand. He was the embodiment of a life learner and an indefatigable worker. In fact, the day he died he was getting up and getting dressed for work when he passed out and expired in the kitchen.

- My brother Ronald Ingram. Ronald is the embodiment of that scripture that reads "Faith without works is dead." He taught me more about faith and action than probably anybody else with Bishops Curry and William running a close second. That's only because since Ron was my brother I got to see his life up close whereas Bishop is my pastor and I only get to see snippets of his life. The same with Bishop William. I knew more about their public lives rather than their personal lives. I knew the intimate details of Ronald's life. From the time Ronald was in high school, he demonstrated unparalleled focus and discipline to change his circumstances. He went from a floundering high school student in the ninth and tenth grade to an honor roll student in the eleventh and twelfth grades. There's a part of his story that involved his dream of going to college being derailed by our mother, but since that is his story I'm going to leave it out here. I will say that with the help of some key mentors and helpers he was able to secure a scholarship to Miami-Dade Junior College. There because of his high grade point average and work ethic he was able to get another scholarship to the University of Miami where he graduated with a bachelor's degree in marketing. By the time he finished UM, Ronald had gone from an at-risk high school student in the ninth grade to an entry level executive with Sears and Roebuck. He excelled in the corporate world and worked in several states for Sears. In in every state he lived in he found a church home. By his estimation for many of those years his faith was not grounded or up to what he thought his faith should be, but by me looking on, his faith was extraordinary. My brother taught me so many lessons and there's no way I can fit them all in. I recognize that mother did her best, but her interpersonal skills and her emotional maturity would not always at levels of excellence. She could be abusive, argumentative, dishonest and had a hard time ever saying she was sorry. Many of those habits injured Ronald emotionally and in some cases physically. Despite those misdeeds, once he was out on his own, he made it a priority to take care of mother. I remember him telling me that he sent her money every month. Not only did he send her money, but she was the first bill he paid. He said if he didn't do it that way it was always easy to find an excuse not to send it. I watched her relationship with him change and more importantly I actually saw a softness and beauty come out of her that I had never seen before. In 2012 Ronald was diagnosed with cancer and given two months to live. When the doctor gave him the diagnosis he said, "Okay." The doctor said I'm not sure you're hearing me. Ronald said I assure you I am hearing you, moreover I believe that you believe what you're saying, but my story is yet to be written. Thirteen years later, Ronald is still here. In a bitter twist of irony, when Patsy, his friend from childhood, heard about what was going on, she flew to Chicago to pray with him. She returned home and died within a couple of weeks even though she wasn't sick and to his knowledge there was nothing wrong with her. Such is the capriciousness of life. Since Ronald's diagnosis he has continued to be an International Missionary at Moody Bible Baptist in Chicago. He's continued to travel the world and has been to another fifteen countries in the time frame in which he was told he wouldn't be here. The man is a force of nature. Intelligent, well dressed, well spoken, a critical thinker, an excellent teacher, and an awesome brother.

An Intimate Conversation

- Irving Thomas Junior is my best friend. Amongst the many things he taught me is that even if you're talented and gifted you have to work to perfect your talents and gifts. At fourteen-years-old Irving was 6'04" and recruited to play basketball from his middle school. By the tenth grade he was playing with the varsity team which typically in the ninth and tenth graders played with junior varsity. I met him on a lark. I was a cashier at the Citgo Quik Mart at 16850 NW 27th Avenue. I worked there so long that to this day I still remember the telephone number (305-625-0475). He came in one day I don't remember what it was, but I think he said that he had come in there and stolen something from the store a candy a pop or something, but he wanted to tell me that he'd done it. So, I told him listen you don't have to steal anything from here. Whenever you come in here just tell me what you want, and I will buy it for you. From there he began to come in the store after school or after practice. I don't know how much time passed but at some point a pretty lady came in to the store and asked me, "Are you Laurick?" I said, "I am." She said, "I just want to thank you. I'm Junior's mother." That's what she called Irving, since his father was Irving Senior. She said, "I appreciate the time you spend with him and everything you're doing for him, and I'd like you to come over to my house for dinner on Sunday." I went to her house and somehow became her *de facto* third son along with the other four daughters and Irving's older brother. Irving asked me if I would come and watch him play basketball. I am not really a sports fan. I rarely watch team sports, even finals and Super Bowls, but he asked me, so I came. From there, I, like his mother, became a big fan and followed him all the way through his basketball career. His father had left his mom, and he eventually divorced her, so she pretty much raised Irving by herself. Senior's absence enflamed rather than smothered Irving's passion for basketball and Irving could already see in his mind that he was going to go pro. Irving's father was a painter, but the man worked like a rented mule. He could fix things, paint, rebuild boats and a host of other handy man skills. He painted the station wagon for his stepson. The car garnered so much attention it got the nickname "The Creation" because of all the fine artwork on it. To my knowledge Senior never came to the single game. Once I started coming, I don't remember missing a single game. I had the joy of watching him grow from Carrol City High School to being one of the top ten players in the nation as ranked by the McDonald's All American. From there he went to the University of Kentucky for two years but finished his college career as a Florida State University Seminole. He made it to the pros and got on with the Lakers. He was with them for about two years when he got cut. From there he went overseas and played in Greece, Italy, Spain, and France. His basketball career ended when he irreparably injured his knee. He came back home to the U.S. and after a time got a job with the LA Lakers as a Scout, where he still works today. I marveled at the amount of effort he put into perfecting his game. In the off season he would go and run with work boots on in the sand up on 27th Avenue. He told me that he had practiced over 10,000 layups, and the list goes on. The main thing he showed me is despite his natural genetic height, strength, etcetera, he never stopped developing his talents and he still has not. I am blessed to have him as a friend. During the time when his high school basketball career was on fire and Carol City was on the way to becoming national champions, my mom took deathly ill and was at the Mount Sinai Hospital in intensive care for sixty days. I was sleeping out of the hospital in the waiting room to relieve my brother Ronald, who was at the hospital during the daytime. With all the demands that were on Irving, he found time to come and spend some nights in the waiting room, while I kept vigil for my mother. There is no better friend I could have hoped for. He is the godfather of both my sons, and I am godfather to his twins Marcus and Mathieu, his other son Jordan, and his beautiful daughter Jazmine.

- The late Tosca Marie Johnson, my grandniece. She had some burdens in life, I'm not sure what the diagnosis would have been whether it was clinical depression or bipolar or something else. I just loved and admired her. I recognized that her challenges were as real as if she had been born as a paraplegic and bound to a wheelchair. Despite those challenges she went on to live life to the best of her ability, love deeply, and be a bright light to those of us blessed to know her.

Those are the people who comprise my two Top Ten lists.

Q: Can you recount a specific event that best describes the values you wish to pass on?
A: The poem that Grandmother Victoria taught my brother Sonny and he taught me:

Drive the Nail Aright

Drive the nail aright,
Hit it on the head;
Strike with all your might,
While the iron is red.

When you've work to do,
Do it with a will;
They who reach the top,

An Intimate Conversation

First must climb the hill.

Standing at the foot,
Gazing at the sky,
How can you get up,
If you never try?

Though you stumble oft,
Never be downcast;
Try, and try again,
You'll succeed at last.

Q: Tell me about a moment in your life when you felt profound hope or vision for the future of your descendants?
A: The days Joshua and Jawanza were born, and I saw something that grew out of the love Kimberly, and I shared, that would God-willing outlast both of us.

Q: When you picture your family's future generations, what image or scene comes to your mind?
A: Each generation reading this book and writing their own story to keep the chain going.

Q: Is there a song or sound that you associate with your hopes for your family's future?

A: *If You Believe!* Sung by Lena Horne playing Glenda the Good Witch in the movie *The Wiz*.

Q: If you were to select one object to represent your legacy or message for future generations, what would it be and why?
A: The Bible my dad gave to my mother and my mother gave to me. Because although I recognize the Eurocentric illustrations, given the time the Bible was published (originally in 1934, then again in 1960); I still treasure my father's message to my mother in 1965, written by his hand over sixty years ago. Now I have a collection of Bibles. May 17, 1996, when I was promoted to Sergeant, Bobby and his wife Delores presented me with an Original African Heritage Edition of the Holy Bible, edited by Reverend Cain Hope Felder, Ph.D., Professor of New Testament Languages and Literature, Howard University, Washington D.C. This version of the Bible is written to explicate that "Africa, her people, nations, and cultures, must be acknowledged as making primary, direct contributions to the development of Christianity." It is priceless to me.

Q: What do you believe future generations might struggle to understand about the time you lived in?
A: How Donald Trump and people of his ilk believe the rules only apply if they are winning.

An Intimate Conversation

Q: If you could send a short voice note or video message to your great-great-grandchildren right now, what would you say?
A: Don't be afraid to *Dream the Impossible Dream!*

Q: Can you describe the feeling you get when you envision your family thriving fifty years from now?
A: My heart swells with the pride of knowing I did something (this book) that will tell my story decades after I am gone.

Q: Is there a family photo that stirs up memories and emotions for you?
A: Two photos are one of Kimberly and me on the beach in Nassau celebrating our 35th wedding anniversary. The other is when I took Jawanza to Josh's school for Joshua's kindergarten picture day, and the photographer took a picture of them together.

Q: If you could add one item to a time capsule for future generations, what would it be?
A: The Bible my mother signed and gave to me and the one Bobby and Delores gave me.

Q: Do you have any final words you would like to say?
A: I close with the words of Mahatma Gandhi: "Be the change you want to see in the world."

Appendix—1959...

An Historical Snapshot of the Year I was Born.

- Facing a popular revolution spearheaded by Fidel Castro's 26th of July Movement, Cuban dictator Fulgencio Batista flees the island nation. Amid celebration and chaos in the Cuban capital of Havana, the U.S. debated how best to deal with the radical Castro and the ominous rumblings of anti-Americanism in Cuba.

- On January 7, 1959, six days after the fall of the Fulgencio Batista dictatorship in Cuba, U.S. officials recognize the new provisional government of the island nation. Despite fears that Fidel Castro, whose rebel army helped to overthrow Batista, might have communist leanings, the U.S. government believed that it could work with the new regime and protect American interests in Cuba.

- George A. Kasem takes office in the U.S. House of Representatives for California's 25th District, making history as the first Arab American Congressperson.

- President Eisenhower signs a special proclamation admitting the territory of Alaska into the Union as the 49th and largest state.

- Ray Charles' iconic hit "What'd I Say," famous for its infectious call-and-response moans—is laid down on tape at the Atlantic Records studios in New York City.

- Lee Petty defeats Johnny Beauchamp in a photo finish at the just-opened Daytona International Speedway in Florida to win the first-ever Daytona 500. The race was so close that Beauchamp was initially named the winner by William France, the owner of the track and head of the National Association for Stock Car Auto Racing (NASCAR). However, Petty, who was driving a hardtop Oldsmobile 88, challenged the results and three days later, with the assistance of news photographs, he was officially named the champ.

- The first Barbie doll goes on display at the American Toy Fair in New York City.

- Tibetans band together in revolt, surrounding the summer palace of the Dalai Lama in defiance of Chinese occupation forces.

- Lorraine Hansberry's *A Raisin in the Sun*, the first Broadway play written by a Black woman, opens at the Ethel Barrymore Theatre in New York.

- The Dalai Lama, fleeing the Chinese suppression of a national uprising in Tibet, crosses the border into India, where he is granted political asylum.

- National Aeronautics and Space Administration (NASA) introduces America's first astronauts to the press: Scott Carpenter, L. Gordon Cooper Jr., John H. Glenn Jr., Virgil "Gus" Grissom, Walter Schirra Jr., Alan Shepard Jr., and Donald Slayton. The seven men, all military test pilots, were carefully selected from a group of 32 candidates to take part in Project Mercury, America's first manned space program. NASA planned to begin manned orbital flights in 1961.

- "First Lady of Song" Ella Fitzgerald becomes the first Black woman to win a Grammy at the Recording Academy's inaugural awards show.

An Intimate Conversation

- Maj. Dale R. Buis and Master Sgt. Chester M. Ovnand become the first Americans killed in the American phase of the Vietnam War when guerrillas strike a Military Assistance Advisory Group (MAAG) compound in Bien Hoa, 20 miles northeast of Saigon.

- During the grand opening ceremony of the American National Exhibition in Moscow, Vice President Richard Nixon and Soviet leader Nikita Khrushchev engage in a heated debate about capitalism and communism in the middle of a model kitchen set up for the fair. The so-called "kitchen debate" became one of the most famous episodes of the Cold War.

- From the Atlantic Missile Range in Cape Canaveral, Florida, the U.S. unmanned spacecraft Explorer 6 is launched into an orbit around the earth. The spacecraft, commonly known as the "Paddlewheel" satellite, features a photocell scanner that transmitted a crude picture of the earth's surface and cloud cover from a distance of 17,000 miles. The photo, received in Hawaii, takes nearly 40 minutes to transmit.

- The modern United States receives its crowning star when President Dwight D. Eisenhower signs a proclamation admitting Hawaii (Native spelling: Hawai'i) into the Union as the 50th state.

- A Soviet rocket crashes into the moon's surface, becoming the first man-made object sent from earth to reach the lunar surface. The event gave the Soviets a short-lived advantage in the "space race" and prompted even greater effort by the United States to develop its own space program.

- Guggenheim Museum opens in New York City. On October 21, 1959, on New York City's Fifth Avenue, thousands of people line up outside a bizarrely shaped white concrete building that resembled a giant upside-down cupcake. It was opening day at the new Guggenheim Museum, home to one of the world's top collections of modern art.

- The Sound of Music opens on Broadway, becoming a smash success from the first night

Afterword

Life Story Concept thanks you for sharing your precious time with us. We would enjoy keeping in contact with you. You can find us online at http://lifestoryconcept.com. If you have enjoyed this book, please take a moment to write a review or contact us via our webpage. If there is something you would like to see changed, please contact us via our webpage with your comments and we will get back to you.

Acknowledgements

I would like to thank my mother, my sister Toy, my wife, Kim, my sons, Joshua and Jawanza. My brother, Ronald, my best friend, Irving Thomas, and of course, my grandniece, Tosca Marie Johnson.

God bless!

www.ingramcontent.com/pod-product-compliance
Lightning Source LLC
Chambersburg PA
CBHW032049150426
43194CB00006B/462